Kiauna Womack

SOUL
SURVIVORS

SOUL
SURVIVORS

The Official Autobiography of
Destiny's Child

Beyoncé Knowles,
Kelly Rowland, and
Michelle Williams

with James Patrick Herman

 ReganBooks
An Imprint of HarperCollinsPublishers

Praise be to Beyoncé Knowles, Kelly Rowland, and Michelle Williams. I have been blessed to collaborate with the hardest-working women in show business.

Additionally, I wish to extend my gratitude to Mathew, Tina, and Solange Knowles for their support, and to Doris Rowland and Anita Williams for speaking with me about their daughters. And thanks to Yvette Noel-Schure at Columbia Records, who introduced me to Destiny's Child.

I appreciate the assistance of the Music World Entertainment staff, including Angela Phea, Anissa Gordon, Angela Beyince, Danika Berry, Courtney Carter, Joe Sutton, Ty Hunter, and Maisha Harrell. I am thankful for the opportunity to meet Pastor Rudy Rasmus and attend service at St. John's United Methodist Church. I would also like to thank Vernell Jackson at Headliners Hair Salon.

I am especially grateful to my publisher, Judith Regan, and my editor, Renee Iwaszkiewicz, at Regan Books; my agent, Eileen Cope of Lowenstein Associates; and Jonathan D. Haft, Esq., of GHLH.

I would like to thank everyone at InStyle magazine for their encouragement, namely my inspiring managing editor, Martha Nelson.

I am indebted to all of my friends and former editors in the magazine industry: Amy Gross, Pat Towers, Elaina Richardson, Roberta Myers, Jennifer Pierce Barr, and Jil Derryberry among them.

Most of all, I want to thank my mother, Theda Costadi Herman, an independent woman in her own right.

—J.P.H.

HarperCollins books may be purchased for educational, business, or sales promotional use. For information please write: Special Markets Department, HarperCollins Publishers Inc.,
10 East 53rd Street, New York, NY 10022.

FIRST EDITION

Designed by Bau-Da Design Lab, Inc.

Printed on acid-free paper

Library of Congress Cataloging-in-Publication Data

Beyoncé.
    Soul survivors : the official autobiography of Destiny's Child / by Beyoncé Knowles, Kelly Rowland, and Michelle Williams, with James Patrick Herman.
        p.   cm.
    Includes discography (p.   ).
    ISBN 0-06-009417-6
    1. Destiny's Child (Musical group)   2. Singers—United States—Biography.
    I. Rowland, Kelly, 1981–   II. Williams, Michelle (Tenitra Michelle)   III. Title.

ML421.D47 B49 2002
782.421643'0922—dc21
[B]   2002017851

02 03 04 05 06 ❖/RRD 10 9 8 7 6 5 4 3 2 1

Beyoncé

To Momma and Daddy, this book is dedicated to
you . . . for all of the sacrifices you have made in
your lives to make my dreams come true.

Kelly

To Mathew and Tina Knowles, who
believed in us. I love you.

Michelle

I dedicate this book to the entire Williams family, the
Washington family, and Miss Breanna Burt.

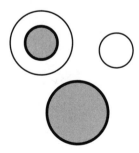

CONTENTS

THE POWER OF THREE

BEYONCÉ: People always ask us about Destiny's Child's decision to remain a trio instead of a quartet. Well, it wasn't really our decision—it was God's. Some may disagree, but He has His way of doing things, and we all just needed to hear and accept it.

It was July 2000. Michelle, Kelly, and I had just landed in Los Angeles from Seattle, and in a few hours we would be off once again (the story of our lives), this time to Sydney. It would be our first show in Australia since the original group lineup changed, when we added Michelle and Farrah, so in a way we felt like we were starting over again. All of the fans down under were expecting to see the "new" Destiny's Child perform. (Well, they got more than they expected!)

About three hours before our departure from Los Angeles International Airport, I was thinking about my bed at home and how long it had been since I actually got to sleep there. (And anyone who knows me knows I can never get enough sleep.) I wanted to take a shower, and the paint on my nails was chipped. My eyes were so tired; I wished I could take a nap, but the nasty airport lighting was too bright.

Kelly, Michelle, and our backup dancers took seats next to me. They were sprawled out on their chairs, enjoying what would be the last chance to stretch out their legs before getting on board a fourteen-hour flight. We were all about ready to drop from exhaustion. We had just finished a long weekend of promotional work in Seattle—waking up at 7 A.M. for a live radio interview, staying up until 11 P.M. to wrap up a concert, and all the time in between getting followed around and filmed by MTV's cameras. That week was even more stressful, because Farrah had decided to leave us and go back to L.A. as soon as we got to Seattle. She told us she wasn't feeling well.

Farrah walking out on us was just about the last straw. We had all met before the Seattle weekend with the intention of working it out with her. We could tell she had been feeling overwhelmed lately, even though she never spoke up in our weekly meetings. During the past few weeks, Farrah had missed some rehearsals, and Michelle had to work extra hard on the mike when it came time for their backup vocals. We figured the long flight to Sydney would be a good time to bond and work everything out. But when Michelle, Kelly, and I got to LAX, she wasn't there to meet us.

MICHELLE: I knew Beyoncé and Kelly were worried about Farrah. She hadn't come back after leaving the meeting we had in Seattle, and all she left us was a note saying she went back to L.A. We, of course, figured we'd give her the break, do the Seattle leg of the promotional tour ourselves, and work things out on the trip to Australia. If there is one thing Destiny's Child never does, it's give up. Beyoncé called her using my cell phone. That's when the drama started—she wasn't coming. Beyoncé was talking with her and trying to get her to change her mind by saying, "We can figure out a better way for you to leave the group than this." But Farrah was still at her apartment and would not come to the airport.

BEYONCÉ: When Kelly and Michelle asked why Farrah wasn't coming, I told them she said she was tired. It's not like she was afraid to fly. I couldn't make any sense of her reasons for not wanting to come. Over the phone I said to her, "Farrah, this is a business. We have sold-out dates and thousands of fans are expecting us. Columbia Records has been planning this trip since before they even found out that we had added you and Michelle. This is a job like any other job, and you can't just decide not to go because you don't feel like it."

KELLY: If you could have seen the look on Beyoncé's face! I knew something was up the second I heard her on the phone with Farrah. Beyoncé was saying, "Think like a businesswoman, Farrah. Be smart." That's the moment I knew for sure that Farrah would not be joining us: I could overhear the way she was talking to Beyoncé. It was not nice. I thought to myself, Oh, girl, you are over! I told Beyoncé, "Please! You know what? Tell her, 'Don't even come to the airport. Don't set foot inside that car. Just stay home.' "

MICHELLE: I was so scared—Farrah had just hung up with Beyoncé. I told them, "No, please, let me try to talk some sense into her." Just then my cell phone rang—it was Farrah.

"Please come. Let's work it out," I said. "Really, things cannot be that bad." I was trying to make Farrah realize that Beyoncé and Kelly cared about her future and didn't want the media frenzy that happened with LeToya and LaTavia to happen again. It was so obvious that they were willing to try to work it out. They didn't want Farrah to leave, but she wouldn't budge. I said, "Girl, you have plenty of time to get here. Even if you haven't packed, you still have enough time to throw some clothes in a suitcase and hop a cab to the airport. Whatever the problem is, it's not anything that cannot be worked out—we have a long flight ahead of us." I was practically begging her, but she wasn't having it.

Beyoncé and Farrah talked one last time, and Farrah said something like "I'm not going anywhere until I talk to management." Beyoncé kept saying, "We ain't got time for that. You have no good reason not to come!" God help us, I thought. What are we going to do now? Then I heard Beyoncé say the words Kelly and I had been thinking, "Farrah, if you do not come on this trip, there is no way that you can remain in the group. There is just no way. You cannot decide to take some vitally important days off just because you feel like you are under stress." I couldn't hear what Farrah said next, but then Beyoncé ended it by saying, "Well, then I wish you the best. May God bless you. Good-bye!" And then she hung up the phone. Farrah had so many opportunities to get to the airport that day and the next day. We could have pushed our first show in Sydney back or stayed an extra day in L.A. We would have done everything in our power to make it work.

KELLY: But, we flew to Australia without her—just the three of us, Beyoncé, Michelle, and me. We were so scared. We realized that we would have to change our dance moves, our vocal parts, and, of course, our chemistry. But Michelle has a really beautiful voice, and Beyoncé and I had faith in her. Where there were two, there was now one—and we knew she could hold her own. Every time we went through any kind of struggle it has always made us stronger. And this time was certainly no exception. So for that show, we prayed backstage and said, "Y'all, God is with us. We're gonna do this, and it's gonna be tight." And it turned out to be simpler than I could have ever imagined. Basically, Michelle, Beyoncé, and I just had to move over one spot onstage!

BEYONCÉ: Michelle and Kelly sang backup just as well as they always had—actually they were stronger, because they were trying really hard not to let the drama get in the way of the performance. The crowd didn't need to see that. The show was tighter and, frankly, it looked better, too—we were all about the same height and there was a great vibe. Not a trace of negativity. Actually, it felt a lot more real. I looked over at Michelle and she smiled. At one point onstage Kelly threw an arm over my shoulder and laughed. I could feel the love around me—and in the audience, too. The people in the crowd didn't seem to care. They were excited, and they were into us.

When we sang the gospel medley, which is a cappella, that moment on the stage is when we knew for certain. That's how it was meant to be. We felt God on that stage. We were comfortable and confident. We sounded better than ever. It was just magical. That's when we realized that we didn't need to try to find a new girl. We had Destiny's Child right there.

MICHELLE: The time Kelly, Beyoncé, and I had in Australia was our time to figure out how we would make it—how we would survive—just as the three of us. We decided that we would love one another and always be there for one another—and our fans. I think that was one of the best decisions we ever made. We agreed that this was the way God intended it to be.

BEYONCÉ: After the show, we had a meeting, and that's when we officially agreed not to bother looking for a replacement. Kelly said, "Hey, the *Charlie's Angels* movie is gonna be coming out soon." (We were scheduled to shoot the video for the theme song in a few weeks.) "There were only three women in *Charlie's Angels*!" Michelle said it was a weird coincidence. And I said, "It's perfect! Ladies, we can do this." We knew everything had happened for a reason. God had His hand on our group, and it was going to work out just fine—like it had all already been written on the wall.

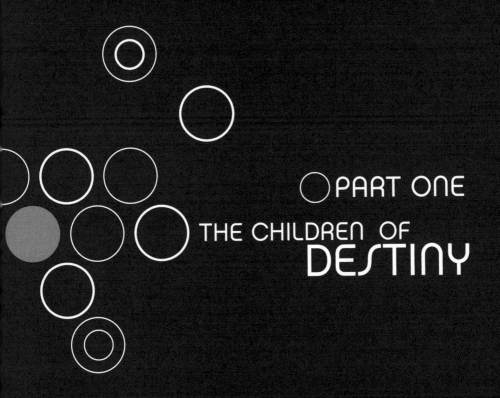

PART ONE
THE CHILDREN OF DESTINY

You will keep on guiding me with your
counsel, leading me to a glorious destiny.

—Psalm 73:24, New Living Bible

BEYONCÉ

I was in first grade when my mom asked me what I learned at school that day and I said, "A song." She was standing at the sink washing dishes, but then she wiped her hands on her apron, turned around, and looked at me. "Well, that's nice," she said. "Let's hear it." I was sitting at the kitchen table, and I stood up to sing it for her just like my teacher had taught me. I'll never forget that feeling. I loved performing for my mom—it was a rush. Even before that, my parents used to sing to me all the time. My dad tells me that as a baby, I would go crazy whenever I heard music, and I tried to dance before I could even walk. He has the embarrassing videos to prove it!

A Star Is Born

I, Beyoncé Giselle Knowles, made my grand entrance at Park Plaza Hospital in Houston on September 4, 1981. My mom claims that it was an easy and relatively painless birth—unlike some of my other entrances. The deal my parents made before I was born was that my dad would pick my middle name and my mom would choose my first name. So Beyoncé comes from her—it's actually her maiden name.

Through the years, I have grown to love it, but when I was little, it was just another reason for kids to pick on me. Every morning when the teacher would take roll call, I wanted to crawl under my desk.

In school, I was the really shy, quiet girl who always looked at the ground and never raised her hand in class. No one would have believed that my mom owned her own beauty salon, because I went out of my way not to look too pretty. I did everything I could to not draw attention to myself. People form opinions of you no matter who you are and how you look. It's a common myth with some African Americans that if a girl has a light complexion and long hair, she thinks she's cute. I can't help it that my complexion is light. I always got opinions formed about me—people thought I was stuck-up. It was not only because of how I looked, but because I was quiet. Some people misunderstand quietness and shyness—they think you're full of yourself. They don't even give you a chance. With those two strikes against me already, there was no way that I was about to let anyone in school know I could sing! That would just make things worse. The girls already gave me looks, because the boys used to think I was cute and tried to talk to me on the playground. But I just acted like I didn't hear the boys calling me and walked away from them.

That's part of the reason why I was so quiet, because I felt like I would have to prove myself and I didn't know what to say, so I would rather not say anything. I would just smile and be quiet.

In class, I was especially quiet. I didn't really talk. I always got an Excellent in conduct, because I would sit quietly and do my work. I was like that up until ninth grade, when I left to be homeschooled. I never felt like I fit in completely with kids my age. I felt uncomfortable with a lot of attention. I was still sociable, but during class, I didn't talk. I remember whenever anyone would try to talk to me, I would whisper, "Stop, you're going to get me in trouble!"

If I got called on, like if I had to go up to the blackboard to do a math problem, I would get very nervous. I was a B student. I would make A's and B's and some C's, but mostly A's and B's. I wasn't the kind of kid who didn't have to work for those grades. Some kids don't have to study hard. I definitely had to study in school.

I loved math. It was fun for me, sort of like figuring out riddles. I really liked it when I could help somebody else with problems, teach another kid the tricks to doing math. I was always fascinated by how complicated it looked and how simple it really was. Something about breaking it down and making it simple was fun and exciting for me. But at one point, in the seventh grade, I struggled with it a lot. I was scared of the numbers—they intimidated me. So did this boy who sat next to me. He used to call me dumb, and stupid, and ugly. I was already shy, and so I just believed it. I wore boy clothes all the time, because I was chunky. He made me feel self-conscious. I didn't know at the time that he really talked about me because he liked me. He had me thinking I wasn't really smart. He would say, "You just can't get it because you're dumb." And if I would answer a question wrong, he would laugh and whisper, "Ha, ha! You messed up because you're dumb." You know how guys are when they like you—that's normal behavior, unfortunately.

But my mom said, "You are not dumb, Beyoncé. We're going to get you a tutor and you *will* be able to do those problems." It was long division that was giving me the headaches. I would get in trouble if I brought home bad grades, because I had no reason to. I was lucky, because my mom always offered to help me. So I got a tutor and worked really hard. Her name was Miss Little, and I was scared of her. She was so strict. At first I thought she was a witch. She was older, and she used to be my teacher in second grade. She had these long nails that she would use to peel apples, and she wore glasses. Her voice was eerie. I was like, "Oh, Mama, please don't make me go see her." But it turned out that she was good. And she ended up being so sweet. She was strict, but one of the nicest ladies. And I ended up loving her. She really helped me.

I went to two private Catholic schools, Saint James and St. Mary's, for most of my schooling. I was really sheltered because there weren't many kids in it. There would be ten or fifteen kids in a class, and there was one class for the entire year—it wasn't like we switched classes. For eighth grade, I switched to Welch Middle School— a public school. I was really scared.

The students at Welch had been in school with one another for two years already before I got there— for sixth and seventh grades. It was hard enough to start a new school, let alone a public school. I was a little excited, because it seemed like an opportunity to grow up a little bit. But my cousin Angie Beyoncé (she's also my assistant) was like, "Girl, I don't know why you so excited, 'cause the other girls are gonna cut all your hair off. You better put your hair in a bun! You better not be walking around dressing cute, because they gonna beat you up." And I was like, "Are you serious? How do you know?" She said, "Yeah, because at my school"—she was from Galveston, Texas—"they don't like girls with long hair." So for the first half of the year I wore my hair in a bun, because I was terrified the girls there would cut it off. Then eventually, I realized that it wasn't that bad. But the first day I walked into class, I was trying to be invisible, because I didn't want anybody to beat me up or talk bad about me.

Imagine

When I was little, I was always walking around with my head down, so I had really bad posture. I discovered that, and many other things, when I started taking dance classes with Miss Darlett, when I was seven years old. She was the first person who convinced me I had talent, so she played a big part in my career. She's the reason I started performing.

Miss Darlett had a unique gift: She could get anybody to dance. Aside from basic moves, she taught me self-esteem, confidence, a positive attitude, and, most important, discipline. We would rehearse every day. She had faith in me, even before my mom and dad recognized my potential. Like most parents, they signed me up for dance classes because it was a way for me to make new friends and get out of the house. (It also gave them some time to themselves.) Almost all my classmates were in my dance classes, but Miss Darlett saw something special in me. She said, "Beyoncé, you've got something. You need to think about doing the talent show." Somehow, she managed to convince me—that's how this all began.

I don't think I chose to be a singer—God put the talent in me. I wasn't forced into this lifestyle either. My parents never insisted that I perform in talent shows. The feeling that comes over me when I stand onstage and sing is just too powerful, and yet, at the same time, I am oddly calm and comfortable. I love singing and performing—perhaps too much.

I entered my first talent show because my dance teacher suggested it. When I went to ask my parents for their permission, their reaction was "Okay, baby. Whatever you want." They didn't take me seriously, because I was only seven. Miss Darlett was the one who worked with me, and together we decided I would sing John Lennon's "Imagine," which is still one of my favorite songs. My parents weren't around when I was rehearsing, so they didn't know what to expect. But before the show, my dad took the time to sit down and have a talk with me. He knew I was too young to fully understand the song, but he wanted me to know what the lyrics meant. So he wrote them down and explained them to me. Then he showed me pictures of Martin Luther King Jr. I paid attention. I wanted to make him proud of me.

For that first performance, both my mom and dad came to my grade-school auditorium to see me sing, even though they were both busy with their jobs. It was the first time I had ever walked onstage in front of an audience. I looked into the crowd and saw teachers, my classmates, and their parents, fanning themselves with the paper programs and trying to get comfortable on the yellow plastic chairs. Then I started to sing. My parents were shocked. I can still see the looks on their faces—their mouths dropped open in amazement. I'm not even sure where I found the courage. All I know is that I felt at home on that stage, more so than anywhere else. Initially I might have been scared, but my fear faded away as soon as the music started playing.

I saw my parents stand up and clap after I sang—I knew they were proud of me. And I remember during the car ride home, I pretended to be asleep in the backseat, but I heard my mom ask my dad, "Do you think she'll get as good as Tracie Spencer one day?" And my dad just said, "We'll have to see about that."

So from that moment on I decided all the world would be a stage—chairs, tables, the kitchen countertop. I made my own stages. That's how I expressed myself—through my music. I only felt comfortable when I was singing or dancing. My personality would totally change—it's still true today. Normally, I keep to myself, and you wouldn't even know if I was in the same room. But when I'm in performance mode,

I become a totally different person. I get really wild. I feel free to sing as loudly as I want at the top of my lungs, and I dance up a storm. I love that energy.

American Beauty

Eventually I started participating in competitions, which are really just glorified beauty pageants. I enjoyed the talent part, but I hated the beauty part, since I wasn't into dressing up. I was more of a tomboy. I wore pants and hip-hop-style shirts until at least the seventh grade. Then I lost some of my baby fat and felt more comfortable with my body. That's also when it became fashionable to have shapely legs.

Those beauty pageants were so competitive. I mean, I know it was a competition, but some people got crazy about it. They took the whole thing way too seriously. Especially some of the mothers—they put their poor little daughters through hell. A few of the girls always seemed so afraid. I felt sorry for them, because their parents were forcing them into it. They looked so sad and uncomfortable in those stiff, frilly gowns, with their hair curled and done up big and makeup caked all over their little faces. But some of the girls loved it, just like I loved performing. They weren't forced into it by their parents—they were just naturals.

But in order to win the overall show, I had to also do the beauty part. And I did like winning those trophies—the crowns were pretty, too. I didn't feel comfortable about getting done up. I had to put on a dress and model in front of an audience. I mean it wasn't anything bad, but I had no idea how to be a model. At every competition there would be a little runway the judges expected the girls to walk on and pose in certain positions. Once I got up there, I forgot all about what I was instructed to do and became a huge ham. I don't know what came over me, but once I got my turn, I'd just strut my stuff and even finish by blowing a kiss to the crowd. When I watch a tape of it now, I'm like "Oooh, what was all of that?" But I won, so I guess it worked.

A WINNING ATTITUDE

As I performed in more competitions, and the trophies began to pile up, my parents started to realize I might have something special. I would overhear my mom and dad saying to each other, "Beyoncé's getting kind of good." And after shows other parents would always come up and tell them, "Your little girl did an amazing job." But my parents downplayed it in front of me and would reply, "Yeah, I guess she did okay, huh?"

My mom and dad slowly began taking my performances more seriously. My dad would spend time helping me practice, and he'd offer suggestions. At the end of my routine, he'd applaud, lift me up on his lap, and say in a serious voice, "Maybe you really could be successful at a career in music!" But he sounded a little concerned too, as if he was almost afraid of it in a way.

Basically, it took a year and a tiny bedroom overflowing with trophies twice my size before my parents got it. Forget about stuffed animals: I had so many trophies, I could barely walk from my bed to the door. One day my younger sister, Solange—she's so crazy—took apart every single one of them! I must have had at least thirty. One was almost six feet tall before Solange got ahold of it. But I wasn't mad; I thought it was funny. I didn't really care about the trophies. I was happy to win awards, but I really just saw it as an opportunity to get practice as a performer. I did it for the experience. I lost sometimes, too, but I never hated the winners. I used those experiences and learned from them instead.

You can't hate people who perform better than you— that's a lesson I learned at a very young age. If another girl got higher marks from the judges, I tried to learn from her act instead of allowing myself to get consumed with envy. That's one advantage of being in a contest: it can teach you how to be competitive in a healthy way. If you dwell on the loss, it will make you crazy. I mean, of course you always want to win, but sometimes you can still win even when you lose—you just need to be able to look at it the right way. You can learn from everything if you take the time to think about why you lost and then change whatever went wrong. This way you can avoid making the same mistake twice. That's how you grow and become a better person. That's the way you have to look at it. Just try your best, give it 100 percent, and if it happens for you, then it happens. And if it doesn't, then you keep trying. I never wanted to give up because I loved performing too much.

Taking Care of Business

My parents were first introduced to each other at a party. They talked for a little while that night and my dad told my mom he worked for Xerox, and she told him that she worked at a bank. So a few days later he called information to get the number of the bank where he thought she worked, but he was calling the wrong bank and didn't know where to find her. (He thought she gave him the wrong bank name.) They both worked downtown but didn't know it at

the time. One day they passed by each other on the street and said hello, both surprised to see the other. They went back to work, and an hour later, they passed by each other on the street again. They thought that it was kind of weird, but said hello again and kept walking. Then, they passed by each other again later in the day, and my dad was like, "All right, look, can we go get something to eat?" And that's how they fell in love and got married and had me and Solange.

I grew up watching my mom and dad work their butts off—and I learned a lot from them. No matter what happened, they never quit. My mom always dreamed of having her own hair salon. When she finally was able to save enough money to open one, she had to work long hours in order to build a loyal clientele. That's how she established a very successful business—her salon was the largest in Houston. My father was the number one salesman in his field at Xerox. He worked hard to learn the needs of his clients, so that he could sell them the things they needed. By doing that, he gained their trust and business. Both my parents were always working, and I inherited my drive to succeed from them. I couldn't help but learn from the example they set.

The coolest thing about my parents is that they didn't sugarcoat anything, even when I was a kid. They have always told it to me like it is. When I was younger my dad would say, "Beyoncé, if you don't want to practice, then that's your choice." My mom would sit me down and tell me, "You don't have to take these voice lessons—it's your decision—but if you want to get better at singing, then you should take your lessons." So I'd take them, knowing that I was doing it for me. Not because they made me. I'm so happy they gave me a choice. They aren't the type of parents who yell, "You'd better go right now or else you're grounded!" That technique never works. It makes kids feel like they are in trouble—it feels like a punishment. Instead, I always thought of rehearsing as fun. It was my time to create dance routines and vocal arrangements. It seemed like playtime.

Because I always enjoyed what I was doing, I wanted to take it even further. Of all the talent shows I did, the nicest was the People's Workshop, a big annual event in Houston that would attract celebrities. It was kind of like an awards show that gave kids an opportunity to get discovered. Two ladies saw me perform, and afterward, they asked me if I would be interested in being part of a group that they were putting together.

They held formal auditions and fifty to sixty girls from Houston tried out. I auditioned and made the group; that's where I met LaTavia. She was a dancer. That group was a different Destiny's Child. At that time the lineup changed so much there were literally a hundred girls who were in and out of the group. It really wasn't anything serious until *Star Search*. Before that, we would just perform at banquets and other local events.

	Oct.	Jan.	March	May
Follows oral directions	✓	✓	✓	✓
Follows written directions	✓+	✓+	✓+	✓+
Behavior matches situation	✓+	✓+	✓+	✓+
Consideration of adults	✓+	✓+	✓+	✓+
Works with others	✓+	✓+	✓+	✓+
Works independently	✓	✓	✓	✓
Initiates work	✓	✓+	✓+	✓
Completes task	✓-	✓	✓	✓

October Comments: Beyoncé has settled into St James well. She has developed a lot of confidence in her ability, however, she should work on completing her assignments in class. When class is missed her responsibility should be to ask that the assignments are completed.

January Comments: what she has missed and see Beyoncé has grown greatly academically this nine weeks. She has moved into the sixth grade grammar book and SRA Kit 2C in math. Keep up the good work!

March Comments: This nine weeks I would like to see Beyoncé focus on her book report writing in S.I.R. and D.E.A.R.

May Comments: Beyoncé has matured nice academically. She assumes responsibility well and has a fine attitude. She would benefit from reading many library books this summer. She needs to improve her reading speed. Thanks for the help I know you have given her.

	Oct.	Jan.	March	May
LEVEL	K-L	L-M	M	M-N
SRA Kit	2C	Color Aqua	BLUE Purple	Purple
Listening comprehension	✓+	✓	✓	✓
Assigned spelling	✓+	✓+	—	—
Grammar	✓-	✓	✓	✓+
Vocabulary	✓	✓+	✓	✓
Oral reading	✓	✓	✓	✓
Reading comprehension	✓	✓	✓	✓
Application of spelling	✓	✓	✓	✓
Penmanship	✓+	✓+	✓+	✓+
Creative writing	✓	✓	✓	✓+
Reports	—	✓-	—	✓+
Seminars in Reading (SIR)	—	—	✓	NA

HISTORY

Work in spirals	✓+	✓+	✓+	NA
Projects	NA	NA	NA	NA

Art, music, motor skills, and religion are integrated throughout the daily program. Evaluation of communication, history and environmental studies reflect the assessment of these skills.

Grade Equivalents of Communication Levels:

3	4	5	6	7	8
FGH	HIJ	JKL	LHN	NOP	PQR

Parker Music Academy
MAGNET REPORT CARD

Teacher: KAPINUS

STUDENT:	BEYONCE KNOWLES	GRADE: 4

KEY [Grade/Conduct]   SCHOOL YEAR: 1990 - 1991

Private Lesson						
Suzuki Strings						
Band						
Piano	S/S	S/S	S/S	S/S	S/S	S/S
Music Enrichment						
Chorus		S/E	E/E	E/E	E/E	
Cindy's Pack		S/E	E/E	E/E		
Orchestra						
Advanced Strings						

I I be-lieve in mu-sic

Please return every six weeks.

COMMENTS:

1st: _[signature]_

2nd: _[signature]_

3rd: _[signature]_

4th: _[signature]_

5th: _____

6th: _____

SIGNATURE OF PARENT/GUARDIAN

1. _Matt Knowles_

2. _Tina Knowles_

3. _____

4. _____

5. _____

6. _____

GRADE	CONDUCT
E - Excellent	E - Excellent
S - Satisfactory	S - Satisfactory
N - Needs Improvement	P - Probationary
U - Unsatisfactory	U - Unsatisfactory

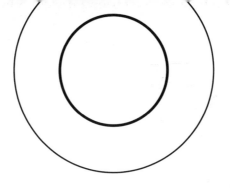

KELLY

2

I will always be just a southern girl from Georgia. I was born Kelindria Trene Rowland on February 11, 1981, in Atlanta. As far back as I can remember, I had dreams of being a singer, but little did I know God was working on making those dreams come true. To this day, he's still working on them—most definitely so. I never wanted anything other than to sing. I used to sing everywhere—in the car, in the shower, in the closet—I really mean it when I say everywhere. My mom used to beg me to stop, occasionally saying, "Please shut up, Kelly."

I've always gone by the name Kelly, even though it's Kelindria on my birth certificate. My mother was the only person in my family to ever call me Kelindria—and that was only when she got really mad at me. She would yell, "Kelindria Trene! Get your butt down here right now!" That's when I knew I was in deep trouble. Kelindria is a pretty name, but it's very long—a whole lot of letters. So when I was growing up, it was just easier for everyone to shorten it to Kelly.

The Greatest Love of All

As a baby, I was always trying to hum songs that I heard other people singing. My mom thought it was amazing how

I could just pick up melodies. She always sang me cute little Sunday school songs, and before I could talk, I was humming "Jesus Loves Me" along with her.

I didn't realize I wanted to be a professional singer until I was around five years old. That's when I first saw Whitney Houston perform on TV, and I wanted to be just like her. She had on a red dress—I don't remember what song she sang, but I can't forget how free, and perfect, and beautiful she looked. I thought, Wow, I want to look like that! I want to feel like that! I want to *be* that! I loved her voice and style— her red lipstick and long hair. She was the pop queen. She just defined beauty. And her voice was so powerful and clear—especially for coming out of such a little body. I remember watching the "I Wanna Dance with Somebody" video. Oh my God, I wondered, how does she get those notes out? She could do all those complicated vocal runs. I was like, Oh, she's sick. She is out of here! That's when I knew I wanted to be a singer.

Whitney had the whole package—amazing beauty, incredible talent, and a strong stage presence. It's very rare that you find all that in one person. But then Mariah came along with the same thing! I thought she was unbelievable and loved her, too. It's funny to think of now, but I remember in the sixth grade I had myself a little boyfriend who was always saying, "I have a crush on Mariah." And I would tell him, "I'm going to *be* Mariah someday. I'm going to be *Whitney,* too!" Back then he must have thought I was crazy—but recently he told me, "Well, you're just about there, Kelly."

The Sound of . . . Me

I was raised a Baptist and attended an old Baptist church in Atlanta. The first time I sang in public was in that church. I performed "I Want to Walk and Talk with Jesus." And everyone there was like, "Dang, baby!" The congregation was very supportive of me. People would actually shout, "You sing, baby!" So there I was, standing on a folding chair in front of everyone and singing—I was five years old and wearing an ugly white dress with my hair done up in huge curls. I remember feeling a little nervous at first, but when I started to sing, everyone was clapping along. That's when I realized everyone there was watching *me,* and I was like, Hey, this is cool. I like this. I was just full of myself! I felt so proud—I had never felt so comfortable. Singing onstage put me in a totally different zone. I came off the chair, and my mom and my aunt were telling me how proud they were of me—their baby sang a solo at church. My whole family was very proud of me that day, and it felt good.

When I was in second grade, I sang "Climb Every Mountain," from *The Sound of Music,* for our school play. My mom says she remembers seeing the kids look at me like, what is this little girl doing singing *this song* and having *this voice*? And she said I didn't even notice. At that time I didn't realize the special gift God had given me. I don't remember that day, but my mom sure does. I guess that's when she knew that she had to do something to help me—*we* had to do something—but we weren't sure what.

Absentee Dad

My dad wasn't around to offer any advice when I was younger. The last time I saw him I was probably six or seven years old. And honestly, what I remember best about him is the fact that he was never there. I can't say that I'm too sad about it now. I don't miss him, wherever the heck he is.

But I missed having a father when I was a kid. Basically, all my dad ever did for me was help me to exist. That's all the credit he deserves, and I don't want to give him any more than that. It's not like he stuck around to help raise me— that's the hard part of being a father. I'll never know why he didn't stay around. I guess he might have gone through some bad things earlier in his life—some people never strive to be anything more than a product of their own environment. I don't know what kinds of things my father might have gone through, but that does not excuse him for abandoning me. I can't say that I'm mad at him, though. I really can't, simply because God eventually filled in that void.

Sometimes a kid who has a single parent sees the strength of that one parent and that inspires the kid to try to be even stronger. If that parent is already strong, just think how strong the kid is going to turn out. That's what happened to me. I had my mom to look up to. Her strength continues to inspire me to this day, and I will carry that inspiration on when I'm ready to have my own children.

LATCHKEY KID

Grade school was rough for me, though. I went through a real sad phase. I would get to school and see kids holding the hands of their moms and dads, and I'd feel very much alone. I would put my head down on my desk and wish that I could disappear. I used to think, What did I do wrong to deserve this when it was not my fault? I know now that it was just something that happened, and it didn't have anything to do with me. Personally, it was a challenge. Maybe it was a challenge that God put in my life to see if I could overcome it successfully. A lot of people come out of situations like that and are much stronger because of it.

I had so many questions about my dad that I wanted to ask my mom—like, for starters, Mama, why did he leave?—but I didn't. When I was younger, I never wanted to ask her, because I didn't want to upset her. In fact, I didn't bring up those questions until very recently. I think it's natural for every kid growing up without a dad to want to know where his or her father is. Mine would fade in and out of my life: I'd see him when I was four and then I wouldn't see or hear from him again for almost a year—never knowing where he was in the meantime.

All my classmates had both of their parents. In school, I felt like some kind of outcast. A few times a year our teachers had parent-teacher meetings after school. I would see kids there with their mom on one side and their dad on the other. I wanted to run and hide, and the other kids didn't help. They would taunt me. I always felt vulnerable, and I guess they didn't know any better. They would skip up to me at the meetings and ask, "Where's your mom, Kelly?" And I'd look up at the clock and say, "Oh, she's coming soon. She's on her way here." And then another kid would ask, "Well, where's your dad?" That hurt. It hurt me to honestly say, "I don't know."

I couldn't bother my mama with problems and questions like that. She already had so many other problems to worry about. And I didn't want to constantly remind her of what must have been a painful memory. I'm sure she already thought about it enough on her own. Besides, it wouldn't have helped to remind her of my father—a guy who was not all that nice to us. So as a kid I was just very sensitive whenever it came to my mama.

Emotions

Maybe that sensitivity I developed as a child has helped to make me a better artist. I know this about me: I am in touch with how I feel. This will probably sound corny, but my emotions sometimes take over my entire body, and it's because of everything I have gone through. If I meet a kid from a broken home and they tell me their life story, I feel like I become one with them. Honestly, kids have come up to me and shared stories that sound a lot like mine. And then I can't stop thinking about that kid. Sometimes, out of the blue, I start to cry, because even now, I'm still recovering. I'm still healing. I thought I had gotten over it, but there is still some pain.

When kids come up to me and they talk about a similar situation, I always tell them, "You know, I was raised in a single-parent home. I didn't have a father, but God will always find you somebody. He is going to send a special someone into your life, and that person will fill that empty space. Don't even worry about it. Just pray."

Bills, Bills, Bills

Growing up without a father definitely influenced my drive to succeed. It made me work harder in life, because I saw how hard my mom struggled to make ends meet for my older brother, Orlando, and me. (He's now married and has kids of his own.) It wasn't easy for her to raise two kids on her own. There were times when my mom would get bills sent to our apartment threatening that she had one week to pay up or else. Of course, my mom never wanted me to see anything like that. She tried her best to protect me so that I wouldn't know how bad off we were. But one day I came home early from school, and there was an eviction notice posted on our door. It said that we would be evicted from our apartment if we didn't immediately pay the overdue rent. My mama is a strong woman. She never wanted me to see her cry, but that night, I thought the tears would never end. It was the worst thing in the world. I don't ever want my children to see me cry like that.

I always wanted to work hard and be financially secure. Now that I have a good career, I occasionally think about the family I'd like to have someday. I want my kids to have both parents—a dad and me. I want to make sure that my ends always meet! Or at least come very close. I don't ever want my child lying awake at night worrying that something bad might happen, like maybe Mama might not be able to pay rent this month. I want them to always feel that everything is gonna be okay. I have no doubt that there will be more challenges to come in my life, but I want the financial part to be set.

Shortly after we received the eviction notice, just when things seemed like they couldn't get any worse, God blessed us. My mom was working as a nanny for a family in Atlanta, and they were going to be moving to Houston, Texas. The family absolutely loved my mom and asked her to move to Houston with them. We had no other choices, so we just packed up and moved. I was scared, of course, but at the same time, I was an unusual kid who was always ready for change. It didn't faze me. I don't know why. I knew I was going to miss my aunts in Atlanta, but at the same time I was excited about going to a new place. Soon after we arrived in Houston, I met the Knowleses, an incredible family who helped change my life.

MICHELLE **3**

I was blessed. I grew up with wonderful parents, in a beautiful home in Rockford, Illinois. I was what my mother likes to call "a bubbly personality" or "a very active child," depending on her mood. When I was four or five, I set my house on fire. It started with my toy box, and then my bed and curtains went up in smoke. By the time my parents put it out, my whole room and the living room were scorched. I don't know what I was thinking. When we would go to visit relatives and I'd walk in, they'd say, "Nail everything down—look who's here!"

When I was growing up, I was always a real prankster. Once in elementary school, I noticed that a friend of mine never had to stand up and say the Pledge of Allegiance with the rest of the class because she was a Jehovah's Witness. Instead, she got to sit at her desk with her head down. One morning I was too sleepy to salute the flag, so I told my teacher that I had become a Jehovah's Witness, too. I didn't think the teacher would actually call my mother to check. When my mom spoke to her, she played along. She said, "Well, please tell my daughter that since she has chosen to become a Jehovah's Witness, I'm going to save a lot of money on Christmas presents this year—because they don't believe in Christmas gifts, either."

My mom realized that it didn't do any good to spank me. When I disobeyed her, she would make me stand behind my bedroom door with my nose touching the wall. That drove me crazy, because I hated to be still. Even now, when I get home after a monthlong tour in Japan, my mom will say, "Why don't you rest for a while?" But I'll just set my suitcase down and run right out the door again. I like to stay on the move.

I didn't realize my love of music until seventh or eighth grade. I was always singing to myself when I was a little girl, but I didn't really try to develop my talent until I got older— I treated music as a hobby. My parents had college degrees and successful careers. So I figured that's what I should do with my life, too. I saw people who were a few years older than me who had gone to college—they were single with no kids, driving new cars, and living it up. So I thought to myself: This is what college can do for me. I decided to get a degree and live a regular, comfortable life. I prayed to God all the time and said, "God, please guide me to whatever career would be best for me." At that point in my life, Grammys were not a part of my master plan.

My First Solo

When I was nine, I sang my first solo with my church's choir. I vividly recall preparing for that performance. For weeks I tried to figure out a song to sing. My aunt Minnie used to always sing "Great Is Thy Faithfulness." So I figured I'd sing that, too. I wanted to sound like her, because she had a beautiful voice. It was wonderful, fluid, and almost operatic. But when my uncle James heard me imitating her, he said, "Girl, if you can remember all the words to that song and sing it that well, then I am sure you can find something of your own—sing a song for real." So I ended up doing "Blessed Assurance." I found it in a hymnbook that we had at home, and I started practicing it every day. It was wonderful to sing in front of my aunt and the rest of the church. The performance was great and everyone loved it, but I was so shy. I wasn't used to being the center of attention. I didn't really do anything as a "solo artist" after that.

I loved choirs—and I loved them even more after I learned to direct them. It wasn't until I attended West Middle School that my teacher, Karen Portis, encouraged me to take my love of choirs seriously. One day in choir class she called upon me to direct my classmates. Before that day, I used to sit in the front row with all my friends and encourage them to sing. I think she probably saw me and figured I should put my talent to use. Miss Portis worked with me after school to develop my directing skills, and before I knew it I was directing larger choirs like the Martin Luther King Community Choir and my church choir after that. Thanks to her guidance and advice, I unintentionally got my start as a choir director. It proved to be a whole lot more entertaining and useful than sitting at home and watching TV.

Choir Girl

It's rare now that I get the chance to sing with a choir— my schedule is just too hectic. But I recently got the chance to sing with the Rockford Community Choir when I flew home for Martin Luther King Jr. Day. It reminded me of the Martin Luther King Community Choir, a five-hundred-voice choir that I used to direct years ago when I was in high school. Sometimes nearly seven hundred choir members would turn up for those performances, and they were all much older than I was. Many kids would have been too intimidated to tell seven hundred adults what to do, but I have never been shy when it comes to my love of music.

I loved being in front of all of those people, guiding so many beautiful voices. I am as passionate about directing as I am about singing. Directing taught me to hear music in a new way. I would have to listen to a song and pick out people's parts, like which parts were for the sopranos, and teach it to them. Then I would do the same thing for the altos and the tenors. It felt good to lead a gospel choir. I got so much energy out of it. I enjoyed inspiring people to put out whatever it was that I needed them to do. It was such a wonderful, but time-consuming experience that I didn't get a chance to sing that often in the school and community choirs. I mainly sang during church services. So now I am sure some people I grew up with are saying, "Wow, I didn't know that Michelle had a voice!"

At home, however, I would sometimes pretend to be Janet Jackson! My mother has a wall that has long, thin mirrors embedded in the wallpaper. When no one else was around, I would pick out a mirror, turn the music up loud, and *sing*. I was about five years old. It's embarrassing to think about it now, but what can I say? I was so young.

A passion for music runs in my family. All my uncles play instruments, and my first cousin Lynn is an awesome singer. In many ways, I've patterned myself after her. There are always certain people in a family who act the same way, and Lynn and I were very much alike—maybe too much. I'm younger, though, by about fifteen years. All my cousins who are around my age are boys, so I preferred the company of Lynn. I was with her all the time and wanted to be just like her. She used to baby-sit me. We would go to choir rehearsal together, until she felt she outgrew it. And before you knew it, I stopped going, too.

The Rockford Files

I'm really a musical person, but the irony is that I can't play an instrument. I wish I could have learned to play the drums or the piano like my brother, Erron, did. One day he just sat down at the piano and played it. He didn't have anybody teach him. So then I tried—*plink, plink.* It didn't really happen for me. Fortunately I can sing.

In a way, Erron and I are similar, because I learned to sing without the help of any voice lessons. I didn't start taking voice lessons until my junior year of high school, when one of my teachers convinced me to take them during my lunch break. It was fun, but I didn't take it seriously, because I didn't have any music-industry connections. I knew that no talent scout was ever going to visit my hometown and discover me. If anyone from Illinois wanted to make it big, they had to go to Chicago first. No one ever came to Rockford—unless they had family there.

Rockford never produced many superstars, which is another reason why I never took my singing seriously. I contented myself with singing at church. Secretly, though, I hoped that one day somebody would hear me, and I'd end up singing in a real gospel group in Chicago. I figured that eventually I could find a band there and sing backup for them—just on the side. I wasn't ready to jump right out and join a group. I never thought there was anything wrong with making a career out of music, but in my family, it was a tradition to get a college degree after you finished high school. After my mom graduated, she took a job as a nurse at Rockford Memorial Hospital, while my dad worked in a printing-press factory (he's a car salesman now). They both worked when I was growing up, but my mom usually worked a day shift and my dad would work at night, so one of them was always around the house.

Beyoncé and Kelly were lucky in the way they grew up. I wish I could have been in the camps that they had—taking dance classes, singing, getting in shape. Houston is a major city, and their parents encouraged them—Beyoncé's even quit their jobs to help out those girls. I would have never thought to ask my parents to help me out with a career in music. They knew I could sing, but I'm not sure they thought it was that big of a deal. So maybe that's another reason I didn't really jump to it.

Hidden Talent

What I lacked growing up was self-confidence. I needed people to tell me that I was gifted before I started to believe it myself. I always saw myself as a plain Jane. I never primped and primed myself to be a star. But spiritually, other people could see something special in me. Some people can see something deeper than flesh. Even now, they read past my hair and makeup and say, "You have a gift that makes you stand out. There's something different about you." And to me, that's spiritual. I didn't make an effort to stand out by wearing flashy colors. I tried to blend in. But thankfully a few people still noticed my talent.

One of those people was Carl Cole, the head of my school's music department. One day he asked me to sing the verses of songs he had written. He brought talent out of me that I didn't even know I was capable of. And that's when people really began to hear what I had to offer.

My mom likes to tell this story: Once a minister from another church told her that all her children were going to be successful. He didn't specify how. He just said, "You don't have to worry about any of your children. They're going to make it. One day they will all be prosperous, and many blessings will come through them." I'm sure that he didn't have the "Bootylicious" video in mind!

The School of Hard Knocks

My faith has helped me to overcome—well, at least come to terms with—so many of my troubles. My self-image, for instance. When I was growing up, I didn't have the latest pair of Nikes that got delivered to Foot Locker each week. My parents had three kids (now it's four), so they couldn't spoil us. But my mom still made sure that Erron, my older sister, Cameron, and I always looked nice. I just had to get over the fact that I could never compete with the other kids in school. I didn't get diamond earrings and Fubu outfits. My mother shopped at JCPenney and Sears. We dressed like little kids should. But I did feel self-conscious because the other kids in school had all this stuff that I didn't. Instead of Nikes, I had to get my shoes from Payless. My mother couldn't go out on a shopping spree every week she got paid and buy me a brand-new pair of Air Jordans. I didn't feel anything negative, because even as a child I still appreciated what my parents could do for me. I wasn't ever mad at them. I never said, "How come I don't get Nikes?" After all, I still looked cute, and for Christmas and other big occasions, my parents made sure that I got something special.

BULLIE*S*

Kids never made fun of my clothes, but I did go through a lot of other scary stuff in school. It was actually so bad that I had to leave. When I was in the fourth grade at Macintosh Elementary School, there were these girls who used to mess with me all the time. It may have been because I had long hair, or because I was a good girl, or maybe they were jealous because I always won the times-tables test. Our teacher used to give us five-minute multiplication quizzes, and I won them all. I was on the honor roll all the time. I had perfect attendance. I guess that I was a teacher's pet. I did a lot of things to help my teachers out. I had good handwriting, so they would always call me up to write on the blackboard. Sometimes I would even stay after school to help my teachers grade papers—in the fifth grade. But a few of the other girls I went to school with were troublemakers.

There was one incident that I'll never be able to forget. It was wintertime during recess, and in Illinois, that was one freezing-cold lunch hour. These two girls came up to me and asked me to play. "Come behind the school with us, Michelle," one girl said. "Help us make a snowman." Deep down, I wanted to be friends with them, so I was excited. They were both bigger than I was, so I had to run to keep up with them, which was hard because the snow was so deep. It turned out to be a mean trick: as soon as they got around the corner, they ganged up and jumped me. They thought it would be funny to push my face in the freezing snow and then pile on top of me—it was like drowning, but in ice instead of water. My face went numb. I couldn't hear. I thought I was going to die. I started screaming that I couldn't breathe and that's the last thing I remember.

I thought they were going to kill me. The only way I got out is because I was yelling that I couldn't breathe. They must have realized that if they murdered me, they would get in really big trouble. So then they all pretended to be my friends and carried me to the nurse's office. One girl told the nurse, "We were just playing, you know, and all of the sudden Michelle fell over. I think she forgot to eat her lunch."

SCARED SICK

I could never eat my lunch, because I would get a knot in my stomach every day, living in fear of those girls. They were out to get me, and I couldn't do anything about it. One, because I don't believe in fighting, and two, because they were so much bigger than me and there were more of them. I was afraid to tell anyone, because I thought that would only make things worse. I already had them following me around school—once one of them jumped me in the girls' bathroom! She followed me in there and chased me into a corner. "You're not going anywhere now," she said. I was lucky to get out of there alive. They would do more subtle things to scare me, too. I would be sitting in class reading, and someone would pass me a note that said: "I heard you're gonna get it after school today, so you better watch out." I'd look over at the girl who sent it, and she'd just roll her eyes.

I was literally scared sick. My mom would take me to the doctor's office for tests. Of course, the doctor could never find anything wrong with me, and I was afraid to say why my stomach was messed up all the time. I was so terrified that I would ask patrol people to walk me to school. Or when the bell rang at two o'clock, I would wait until two-fifteen before I dared to go home. I made sure I was the last student leaving at the end of the day. I knew those girls were out there somewhere, waiting to terrorize me. They weren't going to leave me alone. So in the end, I realized I had to leave. I told my mom about what was happening at school, and she was really cool about it. She gave me a hug, and she said, "Baby, I think we need to get you out of that school. Right now!" The only other school was on the opposite side of town. I had to take the bus to get there and that was actually cool. Before that I could just walk to school or my grandmother would drive me—very seldom did I ever have to walk.

For a girl whose family has lived in the same house all her life, I sure have gone to a lot of schools: From kindergarten to second grade I went to a private school, the Christian Life Center. After that I went to public school. I attended Macintosh from second grade to fourth grade, and I ended up transferring to Jackson for fifth and sixth grades because of the bullies at Macintosh. I didn't mind moving around, though. After I left the mean girls behind, school was fun. The teachers were really nice, and I met so many different people.

Higher Learning

I had a lot of teachers who have influenced my life, but some of the ones who really stick out in my mind were from my high school. One in particular was Mr. Robert Henbest. He made us recite everything from Socrates to Shakespeare— no matter what the play, he knew every word by heart. Once he asked the class to learn parts of *Julius Caesar*—we had to take a ten-line portion and memorize it. And when someone would mess up a line he would say, No, you're supposed to say such and such. He could remember, say, what line 133 was—and sometimes I have trouble even remembering song lyrics! He was an awesome inspiration. He was incredibly wise, and I knew it was because he had taught for so many years. We didn't see eye to eye a lot, because I always had to have the last word in order to get my point across—we were the same, in that sense—so we clashed. And although we argued a lot, and occasionally I got sent out—even kicked out—of his class, he remains one of the best teachers I ever had. He taught me many valuable lessons. He taught me how to write, for one thing. He was a teacher in the true sense of the word. At the time, some students may not have liked him, but now, looking back, I want to recommend him for a teacher-of-the-year award.

There were many other teachers who kept me motivated, like Mr. Stokes and Mr. Powers. These were the best teachers. They were sincere teachers who wanted their kids to learn. They just weren't out getting a paycheck. Even problem kids who would skip class went to those classes. They liked Mr. Stokes's class because he made learning fun. And he never judged you. He would be your best friend. His door was always open so that we could come to talk to him— not only about schoolwork but also problems at home, relationships, or whatever else. Sometimes in high school I was really tired and wouldn't make it to a class, but I never skipped their classes.

The time I spent with these teachers shaped my life. When I didn't see potential in myself, these people did and they helped me to cultivate it. So these are people I'll never,

ever forget. I feel like I owe them something. I wish I could run into them on the street someday so I could get their number and call them. Because of them, life is good.

∫CHOOL DAY∫

When I was in high school, I had an early curfew and I kind of felt ashamed, because most of my friends had later curfews—they could get home at two o'clock in the morning if they wanted. I usually had to be home at eleven. So I couldn't stay out late with my friends. My mother always said, "There is nothing open after two o'clock except legs! What does a sixteen-year-old need to be doing at midnight?" And she had a good point. There was really nothing for me to do that late. I wasn't a grown-up, so I couldn't get into any clubs. Instead, I went to sporting events at school and participated in other school activities, but I never disrespected my parents by getting home past curfew.

I didn't want my parents to worry about me, because they had worried about us kids for years. They both worked full-time jobs when I was growing up, so as soon as possible, I tried to take care of myself. I didn't want them to have to pay for anything. I got my first job when I was fifteen at Magic Waters—it was a water theme park. Then at sixteen I worked at Bergner's department store and saved my money. I haven't asked my mom for a dime since then. I felt that I was at the age where I could work and pay for my own things. If I wanted to get my hair done, I would pay for it myself. Whenever I got a bill in the mail, I took out my little checkbook and I would pay it. That was a load taken off my mother, the fact that she didn't have to worry about me— even as far as college was concerned.

During high school, representatives from different colleges would come to visit. Since I love to read and I am a pack rat, I would get every brochure that I could find and read up on the universities. I went to many financial-aid workshops and filled out my own forms and got grants and scholarships—and, of course, several loans—to help me afford my education. I did it all on my own.

I had a few minor boyfriends when I was growing up. I didn't start dating until I was in the ninth grade. I met my first boyfriend at a basketball game. My school, Auburn, was playing East High School, and he was a senior there. One of my girlfriends went to East. She introduced me to him, and he was so nice. At first I was nervous, because he was so much older. I wanted to make sure he wasn't out to take advantage of me. But it was nothing like that. He saw how mature I was for my age. And my family liked him. He used to come to church with me. He was becoming interested in God and spirituality, and once I invited him to church, he couldn't stop going. But things didn't work out, and we broke up.

There was this other guy, when I was a junior in high school. He was so fine, so cute. He and I were both involved in a program called Black Achievers that was run through the YMCA. We had meetings every Thursday night at the Booker Washington Center. We would watch movies together and go on college tours. We traveled on a lot of fellowships: Atlanta, Savannah, Minneapolis. But I broke up with him, because I was worried that if I stayed with him I would end up compromising my morals and my standards. I kind of felt pressured into having sex with him, and I wasn't that kind of girl. I think he could tell. He still respected me and all that, but I could tell that he wanted to take our relationship to the next level. I wasn't ready. I was—and still am—a church girl, and my church teaches against sex before marriage.

After him, I met a guy when I was in college. He seemed like a really, really nice guy. He said I was goofy. I thought he was perfect. He and I were just friends at first, but eventually it grew into something more. We would go to the movies and church together. We got along well, and my cousin thought we were going to get married. But she couldn't have been more wrong.

He finally told me he had another girlfriend, and I could no longer trust him. So we broke up, and he kept dating her. They got married and had a kid together. I'm happy for them, and they're doing great. But I'm a little bit more hesitant about relationships. I'm much more cautious and aware now. I'm not going to let anyone else break my heart and trust the way he did.

Now, I speak up more and I can be more assertive and aggressive. I've become more stern. If I go on a date with a guy and on the way home, he asks, "Hey, baby, can I come into your house for a little bit?," the answer is no. And "no" means "no." If I don't want to do something, I'll let my date know and expect him to respect my wishes. If he doesn't, then he's not worth it.

Getting into the Business

I didn't know anyone from my hometown who tried to make a full-time job out of singing until the early nineties, when the group Sounds of Blackness came out. I couldn't believe that their lead singer was from Rockford. Of course, she had to move to Minneapolis to jump-start her career, but before that she was in a local group with my cousin that was called Psalms 100.

There was also a guy I knew named Big Jim Wright who became a big record producer. Early in his career, he used to tell me that I have the talent in me. He's helped me out by giving great advice and endless encouragement, and for that I am thankful. He was able to help out my brother, Erron, with his music career.

Erron ended up touring with Sounds of Blackness, because Big Jimmy Wright saw he could play the drums and keyboards. He knew my brother just needed to be around the right people—he needed to get out there and travel and get some exposure for his skills. God makes sure that there will be somebody in your life who can hook you up.

I didn't have anyone at that point who could help my career, so I went to college.

SECRET AGENT

Believe it or not, I planned on someday joining the FBI, not an R&B group. I was a criminal-justice major and sociology minor at Illinois State University. I was interested in social issues, and I also enjoyed the intellectual aspect of dissecting minds. At times, I love to play the devil's advocate. My father always told me I should be a lawyer, because I talk too much and like to debate people in order to get my point across. I am a very opinionated person. Another thing I found cool was forensic psychology. *Kiss the Girls* is one of my favorite movies. When I saw that film, I decided that's what I want to do with my life! But I guess I got sidetracked.

I continued singing in college, even though I considered it an extracurricular activity—after all, I was aiming to become Miss Lady FBI. But during my second year I became disillusioned. Actually, it was worse than that—I was miserable. Every time I would take a study break and turn on the TV, I saw singers who were my age. I liked what I was learning in my classes, the intensity of the criminology field and the way things were constantly changing in it because the technology just got better all the time. But, truth be told, I wanted my MTV more than I wanted to fingerprint criminals.

I knew I couldn't just sit around waiting to be picked. I wasn't going to be discovered in the criminology department of Illinois State University! After a few semesters of college, I made a real effort toward getting a gig singing somewhere. I had always been careful to never burn any bridges—I kept in contact with anybody who had some kind of connection to the music industry. I always said, "Hey, if you ever need a background vocalist, call me." I didn't believe in waiting around to be rescued. I must have bugged the crap out of some people, and certain people who shall remain nameless never called me back. But I didn't let that discourage me.

CLASS ACT

I was still going to classes, but I also called up people my brother had played for. And sometimes I would drive to Chicago and go to rehearsals with him. In the back of my mind I was always thinking, How can I get a big break? I was willing to drive all the way to Chicago, which was an hour and a half away from Bloomington, where my university was. I spent every weekend in Chicago. And I kept a little address book of contacts that is still at home somewhere—it's full of the various artists I was constantly paging.

When I was eighteen I started telling my parents that I was thinking about singing. I was dead serious. I considered majoring in music, but the university that I went to didn't offer that. So I thought I would end up with a corporate job. But one of my college professors heard me singing to myself one day after class, and he said, "Girl, you are crazy if you don't do something with that gift. You need to start singing in clubs." He helped to get me into a group, and when it didn't work out, he got so upset with me. He used to get on my case all the time. He saw my ability. I was enjoying school, though, and I only wanted to sing on the side.

But the more I grew as a person, the more I started singing, and the more I started singing better and better—it was a gradual progression. Finally I realized, Hey, I can make a life out of this if I want to. Even if I had gotten my degree and I started working, I probably would have begun singing on the side, and because it's my passion, in the end I would have quit my job to pursue it. Not everyone realizes their potential when they are young. So I decided that I would leave school at the end of my second year.

THE GIG IS MINE

As fate would have it, a friend of mine named Freddie called me a few weeks before the second semester of my sophomore year was over. He'd gotten a job playing in the R&B singer Monica's band. Half jokingly, I said, "Really? Tell her I said hi, and that I love her music. And if she ever needs another background vocalist, please call me." And I kid you not, in a trunk over at my grandma's house I still have the spiral notebook in which I wrote the words down to Monica's song "Angel of Mine." Just in case, I decided that I was going to learn the lyrics and find out how well I could sing it. It's a very beautiful song. I learned those words in one night, and the next thing I knew I found myself traveling to Atlanta to audition for her.

When I told Freddie that Monica should call me if she ever needed another vocalist, I was just talking out the side of my mouth. I was being silly. But a few weeks later I got a call informing me that Monica was holding auditions, because she needed one more girl as a backup singer. I knew that I had to go down there and at least give it a shot.

Unfortunately, I didn't have the money to fly to Atlanta at the last minute, so I wasn't sure that I was going to be able to even make the audition. But Freddie's cousin Gladys works for United Airlines, and she flew me out there using her buddy pass. All these wonderful people are kind of responsible for how I got where I am today.

Luckily, my audition went well, but there were three other girls who had way more experience than I did. So I assumed that there was no way I would ever get the gig, but still I felt that it had been a valuable learning experience and good exposure. I planned on heading home. Instead, I had people coming up to congratulate me. Congratulations for what? I thought. "You got it!" they said. I was like, Oh my God, I am going to be touring and singing background for Monica. I adored her because she was my age and doing something that was so wonderful—and she was as success-ful as anyone with a college degree.

School's Out—for Now

I did like the college life, and I knew that I would miss it. I made so many friends and we all still keep in touch. Those were years of personal growth and fun times that I will never forget. I actually loved living in a dorm, and part of me was looking forward to my third year, when I had planned to get an apartment off campus. When you're a freshman in college, you fantasize about your junior or senior year when you might be able to get a little car and an apartment. I liked everything about campus life, walking with my backpack, especially when it was cold and rainy outside and everybody had their big coats on, hurrying across the quad, using their books for umbrellas. To me, that was cool. So I miss it—a little.

And here I am now, a part of Destiny's Child. It's like something out of a movie. I feel like a tornado breezed by and picked me up and then set me back down and this is where I just happened to land. If music is what you are meant to do with your life, slowly but surely you will get found out.

MOVIN' ON UP 4

KELLY When I first moved to Houston in 1990, I thought it was going to be all about cowboys and horses. And when I got there I was like, what *is* this? I mean, honestly, it was just big ol' land with dirt. It was very different from Atlanta, which had a laid-back feel when I lived there. Now Atlanta is more popular, one of the largest cities in the country, and there's a big music scene going on, but when I was living there, it wasn't much.

When I go back to visit Atlanta, it's so weird. I see where I would have grown up, and I think, What would I be doing if I were still living here? I guess I would be trying to get where I am now—I would be singing everywhere, trying to get my name out. I'd want to make something of myself. It's just amazing how God positions people.

It's funny how when I saw Whitney Houston, a solo artist, I asked God if I could be like her, but instead He put me in a different setting—a group. I think it's because He knew that I couldn't handle being a solo performer yet. I know I still have much more room for growth, and there's nothing wrong with growing. I have to thank Him because at the time, I wasn't prepared to be on my own, even though I thought I was ready. In a group setting, there is so much love and support. When you're tired, somebody else is there to lean on. When you're not feeling your best, you've always got somebody there by your side. I needed that.

I took my first step toward "destiny" when I became a member of Girl's Tyme. Everything that has happened since that time has truly been a blessing. Had I not moved I would have never met Beyoncé, and we could not have done all these incredible things together.

I remember when I auditioned to join Girl's Tyme there were a lot of members, about seven, I believe—Beyoncé, LaTavia, and some other girls from Houston. That was the first time I met Beyoncé; she was one of the singers and LaTavia was one of the dancers. I was worried that they wouldn't want another girl. I had to audition in front of them and their managers, two women who were local Houston-based managers. I was so nervous that my hands were dripping with sweat. I was stressing out as much as a ten-year-old can, just hoping that it would be my big break—and it was!

Moving in with the Knowleses

I became really close with the group members. We saw one another every day at practice. During that time, Beyoncé and I became especially tight, and we ended up living together. Because of my mom's job as a live-in nanny, she had to move around a lot, and she wanted me to have some type of stability in my life. She realized that the only way that was ever going to happen was if I was living at Mathew and Tina Knowles's house. I was pretty much at that house every day, anyway—rehearsing! So Mathew invited me—a complete stranger—to live under his roof. And he made sure that it felt like home to me.

My mom was so busy as a nanny—a job that involves tending to everybody else's needs all of the time—but somehow, she still managed to tend to mine. However, she always wished that she could do a lot more for me. In order to make ends meet, she had to work her butt off. She tried to make sure everything was fine at home, and she did the best that she could. But it's very hard for single mothers. I know it was hard for her to let me go, but she wanted the best for me, and she knew it was what she had to do to help me. I still saw her all the time, but I also had Mathew, who is like a dad, and Tina, who is like my other mom, to look after me.

I know we have a lot of fans out there who might not have their fathers around. Maybe they have that space filled by one hardworking parent, grandparents, or a nonrelated guardian who loves them. That's what Mathew and Tina did for me. They made me feel whole. In a way, I was special. I just didn't realize that when I was a kid.

At Beyoncé's house, there was always financial security, and that was something that I never had as a little girl growing up in Atlanta. Aunt Tina's (I like to call her my aunt) hair salon did good business, and I was grateful that I didn't have to move all around anymore. I was lucky. Sharing a room with Beyoncé was like a slumber party every night, but much louder. I remember Aunt Tina would come into the room at night yelling at Beyoncé and me because we would never shut up. She could hear us through the wall laughing and giggling. We were always together and staying up late. Our relationship got so tight after I moved in. And that was the biggest blessing I could ask for.

M-I-C-K-E-Y

Luckily, Beyoncé and I shared the same taste in cartoons. We were both the biggest Mickey Mouse fans, so our room was like the Mouse Museum. We had our Mickey Mouse sheets, our Mickey Mouse lamp, our Mickey Mouse alarm clock, Mickey Mouse everything—it was so cute. I remember one night Beyoncé was drawing mouse ears on the wall with a magic marker. Tina opened the bedroom door and she yelled, "What are y'all doing?" When she walked in and she saw the mess we had made of the room, it was all over. There was writing on the wall and on the carpet, too—she was not having it.

I watched the *Mickey Mouse Club* every day. Basically, I *was* the Disney Channel. I was a huge fan of *Kids, Incorporated* and *Sesame Street* for a very long time because they had lots of musical artists on their shows. And of course I loved *Showtime at the Apollo*. My gosh, Beyoncé and I saw groups like Guy, Jodeci, and SWV perform. It was so cool that we had the same taste in music.

FATHER FIGURE

I always know where Mathew is—he looks after me as if I were his own. But it was only about two years ago that I really started calling him Dad. I'm not even sure why. All of a sudden, I just felt like calling him Dad. One day I just said, "Dad, can I go to the mall?" And he was like, "I love that name. I like you calling me Dad." And that was one of the most beautiful days of my life.

He has been a father figure to me ever since I moved in, and that day when I first called him Dad, it just felt like I was home at last. It was a therapeutic moment for me. I feel like God sent Mathew into my life for a reason. He's taken the place of my dad. And I also have God as my father. So I really have nothing to worry about anymore. It's like I have three parents, and that makes it even better for me. Even if I didn't have my real dad, God gave me two more parents, and that's not such a bad deal.

ANOTHER SISTER

BEYONCÉ Young kids are selfish with their parents. Even if you have sisters and brothers, you want to be the favorite child. Before Solange was born and Kelly moved in, I was an only child. I got all the attention. It wasn't bad to have two new sisters, but it took some getting used to.

I loved Kelly from the moment I met her. I couldn't ask for better company. At the time, it seemed like the whole group was living with me. They still went home to their parents' places every other weekend, but my house was where we would all hang out. So even before Kelly officially moved into my room, she was over every day. It was like eternal summer camp. Kelly and I liked to harmonize—that's the best way to describe our friendship. In the very beginning it was hard to get used to sharing, because for a long time it had been just my room. Solange had her own room down the hall. I still had to share things with her, but I wasn't used to sharing everything, like the phone, my closet, my clothes—and to some extent my parents. When Kelly arrived, and the room became both of ours, we had to learn to make it work.

In some ways Kelly and I were like a female version of the *Odd Couple.* She liked to sleep with music on. I couldn't sleep with any type of noise (I still can't. Maybe because I make noise for a living). Kelly was really neat. I was messy. We had our little quirks. It took about six months for us to get adjusted. She may have always been at my house, but that was different from her clothes being in my closet. Learning to share is a wonderful thing. It prepares you for a lot in life. I'm happy she moved in when we were both young—we weren't old enough to be that set in our ways. In the beginning there may have been some awkwardness, and that's very normal, but it was nothing but good times once we got past that.

I felt even less nervous once I started singing with Kelly. I remember when I first sang with her, I was so relieved, because it was a lot of pressure singing solo as a nine-year-old. When I was doing a duet with Kelly, even if I messed up and forgot the words, I could just look over at her and laugh and keep going. I loved the idea of making up a routine and arranging the vocals together. That was the most fun part. It helps if there are other people with me onstage to share the same sense of excitement—and to help me remember the lyrics!

GETTING OUR ACT TOGETHER

BEYONCÉ: I first met Kelly in 1991, when she auditioned for Girl's Tyme. I thought it was a cute name, because we were all girls and it was our moment to shine. There were so many boy bands back then, like Another Bad Creation, New Edition, and New Kids on the Block. So we decided, yo, now it's the girls' time.

KELLY: For about a year or two, anyway. That group ended up not working out. So thanks to Mathew's vision, we started a new group. That was when LeToya came in and the group was known as Somethin' Fresh.

BEYONCÉ: "Fresh" was *the* word back then. Everyone was saying, "Oh, that's fresh!" Just like how "hot" was popular, and then "fierce," and then it was "fly." "Fresh" was the hip, cool word, but we didn't think about the fact that it would go out of style two years later.

KELLY: Then we went by Borderline.

BEYONCÉ: Yeah, but that one didn't really work. We were Borderline for about a week.

KELLY: And then we were Cliché for a month or so.

BEYONCÉ: We just liked the word "cliché," because it sounded kind of... fresh!

KELLY: We thought about all the clever marketing ideas we could do using a bunch of different clichés.

BEYONCÉ: Yeah, we figured we could sing little clichés to describe our style. That was a terrible idea—just terrible. Then we were given the name The Dolls, which was intended to sound really commercial, because we were like little dolls come to life. But that name was even worse than Cliché. (Little did we know that we would really have our own dolls from Hasbro one day!) Less than a year later, we started going by Destiny, because my mom came across that word while reading the Bible. Six months later we were asked to contribute a song to the *Men in Black* soundtrack, so we had to decide on a name for good before then. It turned out that we couldn't keep the name Destiny. My dad went to check to make sure there weren't any other Destinys, but there were about a hundred of them—so he came up with the idea to add Child, which was like a rebirth of Destiny. People said, "Why not Destiny's Children, since there are four of y'all?" And we said, "No, it's going to be Child, because we are a group that represents one person."

KELLY: And that person is God. Only He knows how many hours of rehearsal time we put in! People will never, ever know how much we rehearsed because, really, we rehearsed all the time. Even when we were only ten years old! Nothing ever seemed perfect to us. We were so strict, always critiquing ourselves, which is a good thing, but at the same time we missed out on a lot of our childhood. Looking back now, the hard work has definitely paid off. But it took us so many years of rehearsals and practice.

When Beyoncé and I were little, we would dance all day long, especially in the summertime. During school, we would hold rehearsals at two o'clock on Saturday afternoon and wouldn't be done until eleven or twelve at night. Of course we would take breaks in between, but we always wanted to get it tight. Whether it was finger snapping or high kicks, we wanted every single movement to be crisp. We were perfectly synchronized, just so in pocket, so on point.

We used to practice in the middle of Mathew and Tina's living room. Without a doubt, we broke all kinds of stuff in their house. They had a gorgeous home. Tina and Mathew were blessed, and they had some beautiful art. I'm sure they still have some of the pieces—cracked and broken—somewhere. One time we managed to break a table. Another time, we broke the side of Tina's glass cabinet. Honestly, we broke all kinds of stuff from dancing around and running through the house. For us, the Knowleses' home was like an amusement park.

During our breaks, we loved to play hide-and-go-seek. We had good imaginations, and we used to make our own fun. We made a swing set on the staircase railing by wrapping a sheet around it and fashioned ourselves a little hammock. After that we would take the mattresses from the beds and slide those down the stairs like they were sleds. We used to have slumber parties and put ice down people's shirts when they were sleeping, but our favorite joke was putting toothpaste and mustard on their faces. What can I say? We were really weird girls.

Tina also bought us season passes to Astroworld and Waterworld, where we went almost every weekend. We were supposed to work at her hair salon to earn it, but we rarely did. We had lots of fun as kids.

Schoolboys

KELLY We did not like boys when we were little. We didn't even talk about them, because we were so focused on our work. We were just in our girl world. I didn't realize boys existed until I was at least twelve! Then I would see a boy and think, Oh, he's cute. But that was about it. Now look at me: I'm twenty-one and I can't *find* a boyfriend!

Destiny's Child
"Killing Time"

from **Men in Black: The Album**

Look for their forthcoming debut album, *Bridges*,
on Columbia Records, in stores October.

BEYONCÉ I was kind of late when it came to boys. Everybody else in school had a boyfriend, but no one in the group did. Most girls at school could go out sometimes, but my mom told me that I had to be at least sixteen before I could date. So before I turned sixteen, it was hard. The boys I liked would soon get sick of not being able to see me, and would go and find other girls. They would talk to me for a couple months and then they would be like, "You know, I got me another girlfriend."

When I was twelve, I really liked this guy and we were together, but we couldn't really see each other because I was too young. My mom let me and Kelly go over to his house once, because he was having a party. When I was there, I saw a picture of him and this girl. It was taken at a dance—he had gone to a dance with this girl! She was obviously his girlfriend, and all this time I thought that I was his girlfriend. It was devastating. At the time, it seemed like the end of the world. I thought I was in love, but I really wasn't. He was a little concerned when he found out I saw the picture, but he really didn't care. He didn't like me that much. He liked the other girl, because she was older and she could go and see him. He thought I was too young and naive.

After that I had a boyfriend named Lindell. I was slow with kissing guys. The first time I kissed a boy was in the eighth grade, and it was Lindell. We had talked on the phone for a long time. And he would come ride his bike up to my school once a week. He lived far away, but he didn't let me know how far, because he didn't want me to know how much he liked me. All of my friends had kissed guys before, and I hadn't. After a couple months of dating Lindell, Kelly was telling me, "Beyoncé, you better kiss him!" She knew I was scared, and she wanted me to get over it. One day after school when Lindell and I were hanging at Jack in the Box, Kelly walked in. As I turned around and looked at her, she was like, "Kiss him, girl!" And so he and I kissed, finally. But I was concentrating so hard that I couldn't enjoy the moment. It was really not a good kiss, because I didn't know what I was doing and I was nervous. Afterward I was embarrassed. I told Kelly, "Oh, man, that sucked. I sucked." I didn't tell my parents. My older cousin, I don't know how he knew, but he later said to me, "You've been kissin' some guy!" I got so scared. I was like, "No, I haven't!"

Lindell and I went out from when I was twelve to eighteen, so about six years. I went to his prom. It was nice, but I would have rather gone to my own, because I didn't know anybody at Lindell's school. I had to be home early that night, because I was in the tenth grade and he was a senior. After I left school to start recording, dating got kind of hard. We didn't see each other all that much.

That's another sacrifice people outside of the industry don't think about: relationships. I would tell Lindell, "Okay, I'm coming home for your birthday." And then the night before I'd have to call and say, "I'm so sorry, but I can't make it. I just got a call that said I have to make an appearance." After years of that, the person has to learn to deal with coming after your career, and some people obviously have a hard time dealing with that. I probably would, too, so I understand. It's also hard going out on a date when every five minutes somebody is asking me for an autograph. But Lindell and I still talk every day. He is my best friend in the world. As for the future, only God knows. All I know is that I'm lucky we are still friends. His friendship is very special and important to me.

KELLY I remember the first time that I really liked a guy. I made the mistake of telling a friend of mine at school, and she went back and told him! I was so hurt. He came up to me and he said, "So you like me?" And I was like, "Ew! No!" But that's just how kids behave. If I liked somebody, I would tell them that I didn't like them. Or else I would hit them—playful stuff like that. You're not supposed to do that when you're twelve—you're supposed to do that when you are eight or nine, tops—but I was a special child.

Suffice it to say, boys did not distract me. Definitely not. I did not have my very, very first boyfriend until high school. He played football and he was really nice—except for when he made me mad. That's why we broke up. One of my friends was hating on me—she went behind my back and told him that I wanted to break up with him. She must have wanted him for herself. Then he got all mad at me: He was like, "You want to break up with me?" And I said, "Yeah." Just like that. So nonchalant. So cool. I didn't really care. And that's how we broke up. After that—after our ninth-grade year, which was our freshman year of high school—was when Beyoncé and I left to start recording our first album, and we certainly had no time for boys then.

NONE OF YOUR BUSINESS

Mathew always taught Beyoncé and me important life lessons, such as, don't let boys get up in your business—they sure won't ever let you get up in theirs. That's just the way it is, unfortunately. Men tend to be very serious, whereas girls can be very emotional. But girls sometimes tend to let guys get into their ear and head, and that becomes a problem. I personally don't believe you should ever let a man get up in your business—it doesn't matter if he's a boyfriend or not. I actually had a boyfriend for a while and he didn't even know I sang in Destiny's Child. He had no clue, because I wouldn't tell him. And really, why did he need to know? After all, that was my prerogative.

Beyoncé's ex-boyfriend didn't know that we were in the group together, either, at first. He thought she played the piano! Once someone told him they saw us performing, and he asked her, "Hey, girl, are you involved in some kind of talent thing?" She turned red and her eyes got huge, and he asked her again: "What is it that you do?" And she told him, "I play the piano." She lied, because she didn't want anybody to know about our group, not just boys. She thought it was best if no one except for our parents knew, and it was a secret we were very proud of keeping.

On Our Way

When Beyoncé and I were still in school and starting to break into the music business, we felt that our music was something very personal, so we didn't tell anyone about it. Our classmates could not figure out why we never hung out with them on the weekends, but it was because we needed to spend that time rehearsing. Kids always wondered about Beyoncé and me—we were always the big mysteries of middle school.

Now they see us and they say, "Y'all were wrong for never saying anything." But we know it was the right thing to do. Because whenever someone would find out we were in a group, instead of showing us love and support, they would dog us. They would taunt us by saying, "Why don't you have a record deal yet?" or "You ain't ever going to make it." Or they would tell Mathew: "I don't know why you're wasting your time on those girls—yadda, yadda, yadda." People were down on us simply because they felt that a record would be the only proof of our talent. It took us six years to get our first record deal, and we didn't talk about it until everything was finalized.

People just don't understand how long it takes to get a record deal. They don't understand *anything* about it. Mentally, we weren't ready for a record deal. We were so young—we were still kids, after all. We realized that we had a lot to learn. We may have been very mature for our age, but at the same time, God needed to balance out our situation. And that's what He did. And so we did everything in its right time and it all turned out for the best.

I remember hearing Janet Jackson say that she never stops learning. She tries to learn something new every day. I totally agree with her, because you are never perfect. I wish people could have seen Beyoncé and me when we were young. Our parents were always telling us, "You kids need to take a break. You need some rest. You need a *childhood*." But we kept saying, "No." We wanted to be performers, and we had to prove that we were willing to work hard for it. When Mathew saw that hunger in our eyes, he couldn't just sit there and watch us starve. There is nothing like hungriness in an entertainer—and if you have that gift, then you're supposed to run with it. And if you're especially lucky, you find people like Mathew to get behind you and offer you support. He helped us get to where we are now.

I love watching old videotapes of our performances as kids. There's one in which Mathew is giving us constructive criticism. We were rehearsing a song-and-dance number, and he was saying, "No, that's not quite right— do it again. And then do it again." We felt frustrated, but we looked at each other and just shook our heads because we knew that he was right. Sometimes we would get discouraged. Unfortunately, the most painful experience happened in front of millions of people on *Star Search*. That performance nearly caused us to give up and call it quits for good. Because we lost.

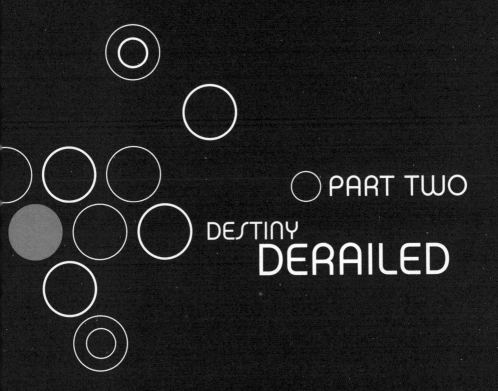

PART TWO

DESTINY DERAILED

There is no such thing as chance;
And what to us seems merest accident
Springs from the deepest source of destiny.
—Johann Christoph Friedrich von Schiller

WIJHING UPON 6
A JTAR JEARCH

KELLY I remember we had rehearsed for months to go on *Star Search,* and the producers had loved our audition tape. We wanted everything to be perfect that night. At that point there were six of us: Beyoncé, a girl named Ashley, and I were singers, and LaTavia and two other girls were dancers. (LeToya was not there because she wasn't in Girl's Tyme.) We ran out onstage wearing the cutest little outfits—jean shorts with satin jackets, two were purple, two were lime, and the other two were white. (At the time, we thought that was cute!) We sang our hearts out for Ed McMahon and the judges—and then we lost. What happened was that the *Star Search* producers put us in the group category, which was definitely the *wrong* category. We ended up competing against a rock band full of thirty-year-olds. They were more than twice our age, and that didn't seem fair. We still tried our best, of course. But as the tape was rolling we found out we had lost, and when they cut to a commercial, we ran backstage and burst into tears. I've never cried so much in my life. Imagine a bunch of eleven- and twelve-year-old kids crying like they were about to die. We had all hoped that *Star Search* would be our big break. We needed a record deal, and we dreamed that somebody important would see us. And somebody *did* see us—and that somebody was Mathew.

From that moment on, Mathew and Tina decided that they were going to help us make it big. They were used to seeing us practice at the hair salon, and when they saw us center stage on *Star Search*, they saw how serious we really were about performing. Under the bright lights and cameras and in front of an audience of people we didn't know, we were still on. We tried even harder, and although we did not win, we got a lot of love from the audience. Mathew and Tina saw that we had what it takes, but we needed help to take it to the next level. They told us we were going to have to get even more serious and increase our rehearsals. They told us that everything was going to be fine. But we had a hard time believing them. We had lost a little faith in ourselves that night, and Mathew and Tina were there to help us find it.

Fallen Stars

BEYONCÉ We almost went crazy from crying—a lot was riding on that performance. (I think part of the reason my dad decided later on to become our manager was because he couldn't stand to hear me bawling anymore.) I couldn't help it. I thought my life was over—we all did. My dad came to the rescue, though. He took all six of us to Disneyland the next day. We stopped crying long enough to go on all the rides, and by the time we left our eyes were nearly dry. We were almost happy.

My parents tried to cheer us up by throwing us a surprise party on the day the show aired. My mom cooked up a big pot of her famous gumbo and invited the entire family over to the house to watch us lose. When Ed McMahon announced that we lost, the cameras actually did a close-up on our little faces—just like how they show the losers' expressions at the Academy Awards, which is so mean—but even then, we acted like seasoned professionals. We bit back our tears and wore like the fakest smiles on our lips, and then as soon as we could run backstage, we lost it. It sounded like a baby nursery back there in the greenroom. I wonder if Mr. McMahon heard us. Seeing ourselves lose on TV wasn't as bad as the real thing, but I started crying again just the same.

After we had eaten, my parents sat us down for a talk. "Y'all can't let this get you down," my mom said. Then my dad chimed in, "So you lost on *Star Search*. That's just one TV show. Do y'all still want to be performers? Is that what you really want more than anything? Because if you decide the answer is yes, are you going to just give up?" We cried ourselves to sleep that night—my Mickey Mouse pillow was drenched—and we thought about what my parents had said. The next morning we all woke up saying, "Forget it. We don't have what it takes. We'll never get another shot at performing on TV. We're better off going back to school."

The cool thing about my dad is, he says just the right things to try and make us think twice about our hasty decisions. Then he allows us the opportunity to make up our own minds. That morning he said, "Y'all worked so hard. Are y'all sure that you want to give up just like that? You need to think about it—think about the way that you feel when you're onstage. Think about your dreams. Think about if it's worth giving up on all of that because you lost just one show." So we thought about it, and we realized,

Hey, we like performing! We really didn't want to stop, so we decided to keep going. It was a unanimous business decision we made while sitting in bed, kicking off our fuzzy slippers. The meeting was adjourned, with a pillow fight.

If at First You Don't Succeed

At the time, it was hard for Kelly, LaTavia, me, and the others to admit to ourselves that we didn't deserve to win. Our hearts had been set on it. But then, when we watched the tape of ourselves on TV over and over again, we saw why. Each time our mistakes became more apparent. One girl's voice was off-key. Another girl would forget a step. Kelly would sit right in front of the TV and tap her finger on the screen: "Oh, we messed up here, we messed up there. We gotta fix these things."

We needed some work. We were good for our age, but that's not good enough to make it in the real world. It's actually a good thing that we didn't win any sympathy votes—otherwise we might not have worked so hard to get to where we are today. We made a pact to improve ourselves. Rule one: Start working out. Rule two: Rehearse every day. Rule three: Get some new songs. Rule four: Learn how to sing a cappella. Rule five: Find some new routines. Rule six: No matter what, keep up the good work. Rule seven: Quit watching *Star Search*—really, what kind of TV show puts small children against adults who are twice their age?

It's not even worth getting mad when negative things happen. I still get sad, but every time that I've had to deal with loss, I have ended up growing so much as a person. And I can only be happy about that maturity. Challenges force us to grow. Unfortunately, since we're human, if everything worked out for the best and our lives were perfect, then we would have no enticement to improve. Personal growth takes somebody to boo you offstage. Life is about taking missteps, tripping, falling, dusting yourself off, getting back up, and working harder to get further than where you were in the first place. It's not worth wasting the time and the energy it takes to get upset and angry. That just holds you back. A lot of girls might have given up after losing on *Star Search*, but we were lucky my father saw the potential in us.

Earlier, we tried to get a record deal, but all the labels we met with were saying there were too many of us. (Only because our dancers were members of the group.) That was something that groups didn't do—dancers were just dancers. Everyone suggested that we make the dancers backup dancers and then the three of us—Ashley, Kelly, and I— would actually be the group. As it turned out, Ashley wanted to stay in school. We were young, and we were friends, and we continued to be friends, but she said, "Look, I'm going to go and do my own thing." That's when my father came up with the idea for a four-person R&B group and became our manager. He helped us look for another singer—actually two, because we wanted to be a group that sang and danced. Since LaTavia wanted to sing, she became one of the other singers after taking voice lessons from David Brewer, our vocal coach. We held auditions at my house to find one more member. I knew LeToya from school; she auditioned and got the part. The four of us were together for two years before we got our big break.

A House Divided

My parents did so much for us in the years that followed. My father actually quit his job to manage us full-time. He invested everything he had in us. I hate to think our group ever put any stress on my parents'

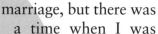

marriage, but there was a time when I was fourteen that my parents separated. I have to remember that my dad was not just my manager—he was also my mother's husband. Father, husband, and manager are three very different roles, and each one comes with its own set of expectations. I was too young to realize what was going on then. It worried me, and I didn't understand what happened until I got older. Back then all I knew for sure was that my mom and I were moving from a big house to a small house, and we went from having two cars to having one car.

We moved into a little apartment, and that's when my mom told me she and my father had gotten a separation. To make things worse, it was around Christmas, when families are supposed to be together. It was such a painful time that I erased a lot of those memories from my head. Basically, I didn't know where my dad was, my mom was depressed, and we didn't have much money. Kelly and I had to share a very small room, and my sister shared a room with my mom.

I don't think I realized what a big sacrifice my dad had made for the group until I watched this made-for-TV movie about the Jackson family. The Jackson dad had spent all the family's money to buy musical instruments for his kids, and his wife was saying something like, "What are you doing, Joseph? That was our savings!" And he was like, "I gotta get my kids out of the ghetto."

Well, we didn't live in the ghetto—our apartment was in the suburbs. But Mr. Jackson's way of thinking in the movie helped me to understand my father better. It wasn't until I saw that movie that I realized my father had the dream of us becoming a successful group because *we* had that dream. That's why he wanted to see us become successful. He wanted to make our dreams come true, and he saw that magic in us. Basically, in terms of giving up his sales job and making sacrifices, he was doing the same things as the father in that movie—and he was doing it all for us. And then I thought, Whoa, that's probably the way my mom feels, too. Now I can appreciate how lucky I was that things worked out. They loved each other. And in the end, I think love prevails. Their marriage is stronger than ever today. Definitely.

My mom is a very strong woman. She is always praying, and I know that God is a part of all of our lives. He lives in all of us—especially in my mom. She has the strength of God in her. Her faith holds all of us together. It held my daddy together, it held their marriage together, it held the family together, and it held me and Kelly together—now that's what I call strong. There aren't many people in the world with that kind of power, but she has it. If you are troubled, this industry will tear you up. The stability and support my parents provided when we were growing up at home has a lot to do with why Kelly and I are still around today.

INDEPENDENT WOMEN PART 1

7

BEYONCÉ We practiced every day. We were serious now. It was the start of "boot camp." At the time I was chunky—chubby, really—so I was on a diet, and I would live on Lean Cuisines. At school, all the other kids in the cafeteria would be eating Ho Hos, and I'd have to sit there and sip soup. It's a shame that a kid would have to worry about her weight, but I was trying to get a record deal and that was a reality. My mom would cook me vegetables. It was nice of her—she tried to still let me eat normal food, but she would cook a nonfat version of it. She would fix me soup and crackers and cut up fruit for me when I got home from school. I would walk in the door and she would have turkey made or skinless chicken breasts ready for me to snack on. I didn't really eat any sweets, and I love sweets. Honey Buns were my favorite. I loved my Honey Buns. And pizza. And Popeye's chicken. Basically, anything fattening I liked. Everything I wasn't supposed to have.

It was hard being that young and having to watch my weight. Kelly and LeToya were so skinny; they could eat pizza and ice cream. But LaTavia and I didn't even drink sodas, we just had juice and water. We would still eat junk food sometimes, because my mom never believed in depriving us of our childhood. But at the same time, I knew that I had to lose a couple pounds. So I would go jogging with LaTavia. My dad would try to make it fun for us—we would sing while we jogged.

My dad was working really hard to get us a showcase. He had gotten in touch with Columbia Records and met with Teresa LaBarbera Whites (who is our A&R—artist and repertoire—person now at Columbia). We did a show for her at the Jewish Community Center. I'll never forget that day. It was the four of us onstage and my dad and Teresa were the only two people in the audience—it was scary. The night before we were supposed to do the showcase for her, we went over to Baby Bee's house to go swimming. Baby Bee was a wonderful lady who produced a couple of tracks for us back then—she has since passed. We all stayed up late and went over for a quick swim. What a mistake that was. My nose was clogged the next morning, because I have bad sinuses. Needless to say, during the performance we weren't sounding our best.

My dad stopped us in the middle of our show and said, "Did y'all go swimming last night?" And we were like, "Yeah." He said, "I could tell, because y'all look tired and y'all aren't performing as good as y'all can. So—I'm sorry, Teresa—but you girls need to focus, and do it again. Start over from the beginning." (Columbia still has the tape with him scolding us.) So we did it again and sounded a lot better.

Around the time we had met Teresa, my dad also got us a performance at the Black Expo. It was a showcase that would attract a lot of labels that were trying to find new talent. Many of the major A&R people would be going—that's where Daryl Simmons from Silent Partner Productions saw us. At the time, he was a production partner with BabyFace and L. A. Reid.

Kelly and I were fourteen years old when we had interest

from both Columbia and Elektra's Silent Partner Productions—not a full-scale bidding war or anything, but we could have signed to either label. It was a tough decision, and I'm glad that we were too young to have a say, because now we don't have to take the blame for it! It was my dad's choice to go with Elektra's Silent Partner Productions company. It was strictly a lawyer-and-management decision—they thought it was a smart business move. Perhaps at the time Silent Partner Productions offered us more money, a better deal, or something like that—all we cared about was the contract, not realizing that contracts could be terminated. Our deal lasted about eight months, and just as soon as we started recording, it fell apart.

The label put us on the shelf, which meant they still had us signed, but they would never put any money behind us or do anything else for our career. We were hoping that Elektra would decide to keep us and sign us directly to the label, but in the end, they didn't. Getting dropped was quite a shock, but being a signed act was a lot of fun while it lasted.

On Our Own

The coolest thing about our deal was that Kelly, LaTavia, LeToya, and I got to move to Atlanta, where Silent Partner was based—but it was also the hardest part, because we were so young and we had to live away from our parents. I guess at the time we were so happy just to have a deal that we didn't let it get to us too much. We thought it was great, because we were all by ourselves. I mean, we had a chaperone with us—LaTavia's mom—and we liked her; she was cool, but there's no one like your own mama. We had a little place, in the basement of Daryl Simmons's assistant's house—all of us crammed in together. We had a couch to sleep on and some cots. We woke up early every morning to meet with our tutor. Then we spent the rest of the day in the studio. We were getting per diems, so it was all about having a little bit of cash and a lot of freedom. We finally had a taste of independence. We were kids, but suddenly we thought we were cool and grown-up.

Before that Silent Partner Productions deal, we hadn't traveled around the country that much. We spent a couple of months in San Francisco recording our demo tape, which we sent out to all the major labels. And every couple of years we flew to California to do showcases in San Francisco and Oakland, hoping to get a deal. As kids, we were too young to really appreciate California—the weather and the mountains and the scenery and the food. We just knew that it was different and far away from home. That was the place to get record deals, and that's all we cared about at the time—not sight-seeing.

• But I loved the city of Atlanta. I told everyone that when I got out of Houston I would move to Atlanta for good. I lived for the malls! We would go shopping on the weekends at Lenox Mall and spend the little money we had on clothes. We knew how to make $150 a week last—we would get so many clothes just for that tiny amount of money. It all went to Macy's and Contempo Casual!

My style back then could best be described as bad. I wore a lot of platform tennis shoes, little baby tees, jeans, gold chains, and big hoop earrings. I wore my hair straight, and that's when my mom first let me get highlights.●My mother lightened a couple of pieces blond—just a few streaks was enough to make me feel like I had something different. That's when I became a young lady. I even started carrying a purse—and it took me a long time to want to do that. I wouldn't wear heels back then, but I wore my platform sneakers. I was still in my tomboy phase, and I didn't like girly things. Still, to this day, I don't like doing things that most girls enjoy. I've never been the primping type. I like handbags and stuff like that now, but I'm not into carrying lipstick and mascara everywhere—I'm too busy carrying a microphone.

Dropped but Not Broken

Even in the wake of the Elektra setback, I wouldn't give up on music, especially after that little taste of a career. When Kelly, LaTavia, LeToya, and I read the letter from the president of the company confirming that we got dropped, all we could do was cry. They told us it was going to happen, but when we actually read it in print, it was like *Star Search* all over again. But we let it go—we rejected their letter of rejection. Actually, now my father has a good relationship with the current president of Elektra, so there are no hard feelings. Every label makes mistakes. When we got signed with Columbia, they had Alicia Keys signed up, and then they let her go. Sometimes people make wrong decisions, but it all works out for the best in the end.

My parents let us mope around the house for a couple of weeks, and that's when my dad switched into high gear. Every morning, he would wake us up and say, "Don't worry, ladies, it's only going to make us stronger. That means we just need to work a little harder. Y'all just need to get a little tighter, but don't worry, it's going to work out." He gave us the kick in the butt that we needed to move on. And since then, we sure have come a long way!

KELLY I hope whoever worked at Elektra Records and made the decision to let us go watched the 2000 Grammy Awards! I remember when we had auditioned for the label their representative loved us. She said, "You girls are very talented." But once we signed with them, basically nothing happened. We did a few recordings, but we never felt serious support and enthusiasm. Even at that age, we could tell that we were not considered a high priority. Initially, they seemed excited, but I guess they had too much other stuff going on, other established artists who were selling very well at the time.

We were hurt when Elektra dropped us. Granted, it was not as bad as the *Star Search* loss, because we didn't get dropped on national television for all our friends and family to see. But still, it was another major letdown. After we had worked so hard for the company—all that time and money—it amounted to nothing. What a shame. At the time we felt like our world was coming to an end. That may seem melodramatic, but we were young. Rejection like that hurts when you're a kid.

I remember seeing the Elektra Records stationery, and I couldn't even bring myself to read the letter. I turned to Mathew and said, "What are we gonna do now?" He was like, "It's all right. Because I am gonna get another showcase for you girls. Everything is going to be fine." He always told us that everything was going to be fine. But we had been sent a letter from a record company that said we were rejected— that did not make me feel fine at all.

Somehow we carried on after getting dropped from Elektra, and eventually we started practicing once again. It's a good thing, because Mathew didn't waste any time getting us a second chance—he hooked us up with an A&R rep at Columbia Records in New York City.

INDEPENDENT WOMEN PART 2

8

BEYONCÉ After we parted ways with Silent Partner Productions and Elektra Records, my dad really hustled. He got in touch with Teresa LaBarbera Whites at Columbia Records again. She was interested enough to fly us to New York. All we needed was that chance to perform for her label. I think they saw our hunger right away and they liked it.

We had to perform in a conference room in the Columbia Records office in the Sony building. We still go there sometimes, just to remember that day. It was a tiny room with couches around it. There were a bunch of men and women of all different races sitting so close that we could put our arms out and touch them if we wanted to. It was that small and informal. It felt too intimate—being that close and having to make eye contact was very scary. We knew that it might be our last chance, so we couldn't mess it up. We didn't even have any mikes, so we sang our songs a cappella: "Are You Ready?" and "Ain't No Sunshine." The Columbia people were nice. They weren't suits, but they were dressed conservatively. It was definitely an intimidating crowd. They looked like they liked it, but we couldn't really tell. We didn't know what to expect. We were too nervous.

destiny's child
4 pack 8x10 photos

www.dc-unplugged.com

For all we knew, they might not call. It was just that kind of opportunity.

The Envelope, Please...

We didn't hear anything for a couple of weeks. We were in my mom's hair salon when we found out about the deal. After church, we always ate at Luby's cafeteria. My mom and dad decided to try to trick us by putting our Columbia contract in a Luby's envelope—that's what they handed to us girls. We thought it was a gift certificate or something. When we saw it was a recording contract, we started screaming and crying right in the middle of the salon. The ladies with their heads under the dryers looked at us like we were crazy, because they couldn't hear what all the yelling was about. We ran all around the shop, jumping up and down, holding our contract in the air for all the customers to see. It was a beautiful day at the beauty salon, that's for sure!

For the Record

KELLY After we did our very informal showcase for the Columbia staff, we all started saying our prayers as soon as we left the room. We didn't want to be rejected again! So we had walked into the audition with our heads up high, we smiled with confidence, and we sang and danced the best we could. I think they were so impressed that they decided to sign us almost on the spot, but I didn't want to get my hopes up too high. That day in the beauty salon when we received our contract was the best day of our lives. We started working right away on our first album. It was 1996 when we were signed up, and we finished our album in 1998. It took two whole years, but that's because we wanted to get it right.

We went to school all the way up to the eighth grade, got a little taste of ninth grade, but that was just half of the year. We left school in January of our ninth-grade year and from then on we had tutors. And tutoring was okay, but it was always high-impact learning. Recess was not an option. We would focus on one subject and not get any breaks—or social life. But for us, it was just about learning as much as possible as quickly as possible. And in between tutoring sessions, we were trying to record our album. We knew that it was important to be well-educated ladies, because the music business is, after all, a business. And we wanted to prepare ourselves for the future. Thanks to our tutor, we finished high school about two years ago—2000 was our last "year" of high school.

Why did it take us so long to finish our album? Because it was our debut album and we wanted it to be perfect. But when you're recording your first album and you're all of fourteen years old, you don't know exactly *how* to get it right. We were thinking about our sound, our image, our marketing strategy—basically, we were thinking about anything and everything. Our biggest concern was our sound, because we wanted a fresh sound that would stick out. Ultimately we ended up with too many sounds—there were about five different ones on the first album. That didn't put us in a specific category or make us seem unique. It only made people confused.

YEƧ, YEƧ, YEƧ

People loved it when we dropped the single "No, No, No." They liked how Beyoncé and the rest of us sang fast. The beat was hot and the song did well. I loved that sound, which was a happy accident. What happened was, we went back into the studio with Wyclef Jean so that he could remix "No, No, No," but we were already over budget with the album, and recording-studio time can cost more than a hotel room at the Four Seasons—it's thousands of dollars an hour. So there we were running out of studio time (and money), Wyclef was in the control room, and Beyoncé was on the mike laying down vocals to the chorus. Wyclef said something like, "Hurry up, girl," and Beyoncé was in a goofy mood. She goes, "How's this?," and she sang the line so fast, almost like she was an MC. Because Wyclef is a genius, he knew it was hot. He was like, "Hey, do that again." And he was right—it was hot! Our mistake was that we followed it up with a song that featured another hip-hop artist rather than the Master P version (Master P was the hottest rapper at the moment), which we had also recorded. I'm sure people thought, "What happened?" So the second single didn't do as well as the first one, which had sold more than three million copies and helped the album go gold.

BEYONCÉ The first song of ours that we ever heard on the radio was "No, No, No." I used to pick Solange up every day after school on my way back from rehearsals. Kelly and I were in the Ford Explorer that my mom had bought me as a birthday present and we were listening to 97.9, our favorite Houston radio station. I had just pulled up to the school when our song came on the radio. We turned the volume up as loud as it would go and started running around the car singing along. The bell had just rung and my sister was walking out of class with her friends. She was looking at me like she was going to beat me up. "What's wrong with you?" she shouted as she walked over to us. When she got closer to the car, she heard the song playing and she dropped her bag and books and started running around the car, too. It was a really cool experience.

KELLY When it came time to work on our second album, we sat down together and wrote down all the things that we didn't like about the last album and all the things that we did like. Next we got a producer named She'kspere—no relation to the author—who had a very unique sound that could help put us on the map. He collaborated with Kandi fom Xscape, who is a very talented songwriter. We also decided we would have more input on the album and write some of the songs. Then we went into the studio. When we came back out a few months later, we had songs like "Bills, Bills, Bills" and "Bugaboo." Then we broke out big time with "Say My Name," which Rodney Jerkins produced. That one showcased some seriously fast vocals—it was almost like a cross between rapping and singing. Then there was "Jumpin' Jumpin'," which was Beyoncé's first time having major writer and producer input. People were like, What *is* this? We had a lot of those fast-sung songs and a whole bunch of unforgettable lyrics and people loved that combination. After all, *The Writing's on the Wall* went on to sell ten million and counting. It was basically just a party album, but, hello—ten million people came! That's a big party. In the record business, it's practically Mardi Gras.

DESTINY'S STYLE

When Columbia signed us, the reps told us they loved our look, but then they asked Beyoncé, LaTavia, LeToya, and me to "enhance our image—just a little bit." Before we knew what was happening, they had hired a fleet of makeup artists and stylists for our first photo shoot. We looked terrible. The clothes just weren't us. They were too trendy. Fortunately, Tina came to our rescue.

We didn't really become Destiny's Child image-wise until the success of "No, No, No." That was the first time Tina made clothes for us. We were filming MTV's spring break in Jamaica. Wyclef saw the outfits that Aunt Tina made, and he said something like, "Yo, that's how y'all need to dress all the time. It's different, it's unique, and oh, it's hot." And the outfits were hot. My aunt Tina knew what she was doing. Wyclef knows about style. He understands the role that image plays—it impacts sales.

For the MTV appearance, Tina had made us these army fatigue outfits—let me add that this was long before camouflage became trendy. She made a pair of shorts, a skirt, overalls, and some big baggy pants. Beyoncé, LaTavia, LeToya, and I each had our own look. Aunt Tina also made matching tops—they covered our stomachs but showed off our shoulders. Everyone loved our clothes. All night we kept hearing, "Those outfits are the bomb!" The stylist Columbia hired didn't know anything about our individual personalities. To me, an important part of being a stylist is studying someone's personality and then making it really pop with the clothes that are selected for him or her to wear. Tina knows how to do that. She knows our strengths and weaknesses and always makes us look great. Somehow she finds time to make our hair pop, too—she's a visionary who takes care of our look from head to heels.

I'm not a natural redhead, but I feel like one now. The day she first suggested putting red streaks in my hair, I looked at her like she was crazy. I was skeptical, to say the least. I said, "Oh, I don't know about that idea, Miss Tina." But by the end of the day, she managed to talk me into it. She put a few streaks in my hair, and I liked it. I said, "Let's maybe put another one here. And how about another one there?" Before I knew it, I was a full-on redhead. The only bad thing about my red hair is, it's almost impossible to go incognito anywhere. I can walk into a mall anywhere in the U.S., and a fan could be a mile away down at the other end and they'll yell, "Kelly!" It still surprises me. Tina says that redheads are expected to be sassy and bold. Is that really what the world thinks? My gosh, I am not sure if I can live up to those expectations.

BITTER/WEET /UCCE// 9

KELLY As I mentioned earlier, when I first moved to Houston it was LaTavia who introduced me to Girl's Tyme. And then about a year or two later, LeToya auditioned and became a member of the new group, which started out as Somethin' Fresh and we renamed it Destiny's Child. We worked together for years trying to make it, and for the most part we did. Then about three years ago, when they left the group, the media had a field day spreading stories about us all. Rumors flew, lawsuits came up, and, most of all, feelings got hurt. It took a long time for Beyoncé and me to come to terms with all that went on. We are finally doing okay—so we are not about to start opening those old wounds now.

We are not the type of girls who gossip or blast anyone.

And because LeToya and LaTavia are no longer in the group, there's really not much we can say about them. As for what was reported in all the papers about their involvement with the R&B group Jagged Edge—those guys are our Columbia Records label mates, so we would never say anything negative about them.

I know *I've* had enough drama to last me a lifetime. I have no desire to get involved in any more legal action. I am a singer, not a lawyer. I would rather spend my hours onstage or in the studio than in a courthouse. I don't want this situation to get any worse. I just want it to be over. Even if Beyoncé and I wanted to try to dispel the media's rumors and explain what really happened, some people still wouldn't get it. In order to fully comprehend what happened, you had to live through it. At the end of the day, people are going to believe whatever they want to believe. A lot of people know exactly what went down, and they're the ones who know that Mathew is a nice guy and a fair manager.

Do unto Others

BEYONCÉ I have let it go, and I have moved on—and the further away from it I get, the happier I am. If the press or anyone else wants to spread lies about Kelly and me, then that's their business. I have no doubt that God will deal with them in time.

My role in Destiny's Child has always been the peacemaker. I have never been the type to start any drama. And contrary to some people's beliefs, I am not a person whose butt you have to kiss in order to stay in the group. When members have tried to leave, I was the one saying, "No, no, no." My motto has always been "Let's work it out." I would try desperately to hold everything together and make it work. I've even made excuses for other people and lied for them. I just want peace. That's how I am.

I do not dis anyone. Not even the people who dis me. I don't get mad at them; I just don't go out of my way to try to make them like me. I accept it. I'm very professional. I can be on the same tour bus with another singer who doesn't like me, even though it's not pleasant. You cannot reach a certain level of success without encountering a lot of negativity. I go about my business, working, doing my thing. I hate drama. I always have, and I always will. I have already been through enough of it to last me two careers.

This business is tough enough without drama. Drama makes for additional, unnecessary stress. And it drives me crazy. I am what you might call a hypersensitive person. If somebody hurts, I can feel it. When someone is crying, I will start to cry even harder. I've always been like that, and I don't know why. It's not a good thing. Sometimes I can't sleep at night. I'm thinking about certain people and the things they've gone through in their lives. It gets to me so much; I can't shake it.

I know how fortunate I have been. I have never experienced any type of serious abuse—physically, mentally, or verbally. Sure, I've had people tell lies about me and criticize me, and that's been rough, but it's not nearly as bad as the suffering some kids endure. A lot of people were damaged when they were children, and that's why they turn out the way they do. I sympathize with them. I feel their hurt. I can see the pain in their eyes. That's why I pray for wisdom every night, but it seems like the wiser I get, the more it hurts.

People have got the wrong idea about me. I shouldn't even have to explain myself, but I guess I need to because obviously a lot of people still have misconceptions. I can't believe how many people have come up to me after they spent some time around us and said, "I feel so stupid. I had a totally different idea about all y'all, especially you, Beyoncé. I always thought you were a bitch."

That kills me, because I'm always trying to help people, not hurt them. When the former members were in the group, I would do everything in my power to make sure everyone had an opportunity to shine. I would literally stand with them and hold their hands in the studio if they wanted me to. That's why it's very frustrating and disappointing when people think I try to monopolize the mike. I am the one who produced the songs that the former members sang lead on. I was the one who suggested it to the album's producer. The producer said to me, "If you want them to sing lead, then you need to produce their vocals." So I did. I sang lead on enough songs; I wanted to give it a break. Honestly, I felt like, Why do I always have to sing lead? It's supposed to be a group. I don't have to be the center of attention. It puts a lot of pressure on me.

I've learned that when you're nice to people who envy you, they dislike you even more, which is frightening. I've met people who didn't like me, and I've never done anything to them. They scowl at me like they are determined to make me mad, and I just smile back at them. I pray for those people and feel sorry for them, because obviously they are not happy and have low self-esteem.

Success Stories

You can't see eye to eye with someone who does not want to air their differences openly and directly. We tried everything to make it work with LaTavia and LeToya—they were our friends. When traveling, we would alternate hotel rooms so that we would all get to spend time with one another. (At that time we didn't have money to have our own private room.) We had weekly meetings with Yvette, our youth minister at church. That didn't help. For twelve months we attempted to work out our differences, but there were problems way before that. We have a whole stack of letters that show we tried to work things out. There were little problems that cropped up, but we always tried to fix them on our own and always seemed to be the ones to compromise.

In truth, our problems had a lot to do with money. Once you get money involved in anything, it gets crazier. In the beginning, when we were all so ambitious and shared the same dream of becoming big stars, it was much easier to get along. We were just starting out, so we had nothing to lose. It's once someone has something to lose that he or she becomes paranoid. That's when it gets harder to trust people, and there is always someone waiting to take advantage of that person or situation. When a group starts becoming successful, there are always people who aren't happy for them. They start attacking the members and try to find ways to pit them against one another, hoping that the group will break up.

Success is the real test of a friendship, because along with success comes money, and with money comes problems. Once you have a little bit of money, more people start to enter the picture. Your friends start to get in your ear telling you one thing, then guys try to talk to you and get in your ear and tell you something else, and then you get industry people in your ear with a different story. Next thing you know you don't know who to believe—many times they are all telling you lies. And if you're not careful, you might start to believe them.

The same person who would come up to Kelly and say, "Why does Beyoncé get to sing all of the songs?" is inevitably the same person who, as soon as Kelly turned around, would approach me and say, "Why do you stay in Destiny's Child? You have to split all the money three ways but you're doing all of the work. Why don't you just go solo?" So if you are insecure about yourself and insecure about the other members in your group, then things like that will start to get to you. You have to be smarter than that.

Once Destiny's Child started to get successful, that's when we found out who our friends really were. Our whole world changed, and that makes friendship way more complicated—especially with females. I hate to say this, but women are too competitive—they let it make them crazy. A lot of the time when we were younger, that competitive instinct—jealousy and envy—got so out of control that it was scary. It can sometimes make some people do crazy things.

Women are highly emotional. And because of that, at times we can't make rational decisions—we don't always think straight. I have learned to think with my mind and not with my heart. That's why it's called thinking! Your heart can't just lead you around all the time. That's not smart. I get hurt, too, but I try my best to be rational for as long as I can.

If you want to be successful in a business, you need talent; you can't rely on your looks to get you far—unless, of course, you work in the modeling industry. In the music industry, sometimes there are people who think looking pretty and dancing is all it's about. Those are the people who become jealous when they realize they can't really sing—it makes them mad. It's easier for them to hate someone who's successful than it is for them to look at themselves.

I don't try to compete with any of my friends. I certainly don't hate on them. I am secure with what I got, so I don't feel uncomfortable around anybody. God is generous and gives everyone his or her own gifts. That means we all have limitations, too. You have to accept the fact that you're not perfect. For one thing, I am not the best public speaker—or the best at a lot of things. I might not be the finest, or the slimmest, but I'm not envious of those people who are. You should never compare yourself to other people. Don't compete with anyone other than yourself.

For example, Kelly and Michelle don't resent me, because they've got their own stuff going for them. If you cut off the music and ask either one to sing, they will blow you away. And that only helps us when we are working together. We all have strengths and weaknesses, but what one of us can't do, the other can. It's all about finding the right person for the job.

The way to succeed is to keep focused. Sometimes young women don't think about the future—they don't try to see the big picture—and that's not very smart. You have to think about your career, set your priorities, and stick to them. Don't let other people influence you. Be careful, because some of the people offering you advice may not really be your friends—they may have ulterior motives. Girls can lose sight of their priorities when they meet a guy who throws them off focus. It's important to stick to your goals. I think that's why Kelly, Michelle, and I excel. When we're doing something, we don't let other people get in our way. It's hard to stay focused all the time, but you have to keep your eye on the prize if you want to win it.

The ∫plit

When we were having problems with LaTavia and LeToya, I was so stressed that my face broke out all over. Lindell and I had just broken up. My hair was breaking off because of the coloring. I was unhappy. I hated the way I looked. I hated everything that was going on. There was so much tension in my house, because my whole house was Destiny's Child. It was crazy. I stayed in my room for a week. I couldn't talk. I didn't have Lindell to lean on anymore. Then the group split. I was feeling ugly. I never had problems before with my skin. I couldn't figure out why it was. I thought, Am I going through puberty or what? I went into a kind of depression.

I went to a dermatologist and that didn't help much. We were on tour in Europe. My skin wasn't terrible, but to be in the public eye, it was bad. I was like, How am I going to go anywhere? (Thank God for makeup.) I was never the type to take care of my skin because I never had to—I was really lucky—but then I was trying everything. No medicine could get rid of my zits, so it must have been all the stress. After I had worked out my personal problems, my skin got clearer than it had ever been. It just glowed. But I became an entirely different person after that—not just a clear complexion. My whole way of thinking and dealing with things changed.

What helped me get out of my depression was church. That's when I realized: It's going to be okay. God's going to make it okay. The church service spoke to me. God spoke to me. It's crazy how it happened. First, the Saturday before the service, I had a dream that I talked to God. His face was blurred. I just saw white light. I asked Him a bunch of questions but when I woke up I didn't remember any of the answers that He gave me. The next day in church all of my questions were answered in the service. My questions were personal: What should I do about life? How should I act? How can I become a better person? I can ask God anything—even questions about a guy and if he is right for me. In that service, my main question was about forgiveness.

Forgiveness is a big part of Christianity and most people don't do that. I realized that I had to forgive—and I had to accept the fact that everybody is different. My first step was letting it go and giving my problems to God. I imagined myself walking up to Him and just handing it all over. And I did. That was also the first and only day that I spoke in tongues. (I want to again, and I know that when I'm ready God will allow it.) That day I felt God. I got really hot all over. I felt like I was going to pass out. I got so happy that I couldn't control myself. It's unbelievable and utterly indescribable. It was the happiest I have ever been in my life. I was crying and shaking because it was so overwhelming. I just started saying stuff. I don't know what I was saying. I didn't make a scene, because I was over in the corner of the church. But people knew. People know when somebody is feeling that. My mom was on one side of me and Kelly was on the other. It was amazing and beautiful.

I talked to LeToya and LaTavia afterward, because we had a meeting with the youth counselor. I hugged them for like ten minutes each and told them, "I'm sorry, and I forgive you. It's going to be okay." And they didn't know what was wrong with me—they probably thought I was crazy, since they weren't at the church service. Imagine seeing me running after them and hugging them tight for ten minutes— I wouldn't let them go. I was boo-hooing and crying. I just kept saying, "I'm sorry, and I forgive you and it's going to be okay," over and over again. I'm lucky because Kelly never got that chance, but I don't think the situation affected her in the same way. I am very blessed that I got a chance to let it all go.

So, it's not like we just got mad one day and decided to boot somebody out of the group. There were problems between us that led up to the split. That's why it hurts when people joke, "Did y'all kick somebody out this week?" First of all, it's been about three years. It's not cute anymore. How long do Kelly, Michelle, and I have to be together to prove that it's for good? I mean, who in the world wants to do videos and photo shoots—a whole press campaign—with people only to have them leave, and then have to go through the press campaign all over again? Does anyone seriously think that would be enjoyable for us? That's ridiculous. It's about as fun as a messy divorce. Nobody wants to go through that.

At the time of the split, we had a lot of promotional appearances to do because we were just starting to make a name for ourselves. We were also scheduled to shoot the "Say My Name" video in two weeks. So not only did we need to find someone quickly, but we needed to find two girls who looked similar to LaTavia and LeToya—we didn't want the drama to overshadow what people thought about our music. We just didn't want the press making a big deal out of the split. So much for that!

DRAMA 101 10

BEYONCÉ It must be a part of human nature to love drama. We never would have sold as many records—and we never would have been this popular—if those member changes did not happen. Up until that point, we were squeaky-clean nice girls who grew up in Texas. We had all been together for years—lifelong friends since childhood. We couldn't get on the covers of any magazines. I guess the media felt our story was too boring. Then two members were gone, and soon all eyes were on us. If you had asked me then what was going to happen next or how we were going to confront the problem of missing members, I would have looked at you with a blank face and said, "I have no idea." None of us did. We didn't know if people would laugh at us and think we were stupid (some did). We had no idea if the public was going to accept us once we changed. Everything was so uncertain.

Video Games

There was no way of predicting how things would play out, especially with the video for "Say My Name," which was the first to feature Michelle and Farrah. But it became the most requested video on The Box, which was sort of like MTV's *Total Request Live,* but it took requests 24/7.

We tried to think everything through as much as possible when it came to replacing LaTavia and LeToya. As I explained earlier, we didn't really want people to focus on the lineup change, so we had to be careful not to make the replacements obvious. When we were looking for new members, we were up front about that. We auditioned as many girls as possible, and found two who we really liked—Michelle and Farrah. We said to them, "Look, if you want to be in the group, you're going to have to be willing to dye your hair. At least for just like six months, and then you can probably get out of it." They were fine with that, so we got down to business.

It was only a week before we had to shoot the video. We learned the routine two days before. When it was time to start filming, we didn't even know if the two new girls would be in the group for good. We just knew that if we didn't film the video that week, we were not going to have any video at all. So we put Michelle and Farrah in the video with three other dancers. That way, you couldn't tell which ones were the new girls. It was a smart idea, and it worked. We put the video out there, but it only added to the drama.

The next thing we knew everybody wanted to put us on the cover of their magazines. Everybody wanted to talk about it—two girls out of the band, two more come in. And yes, it was something to talk about. The music industry, the radio, and the press suddenly deemed us newsworthy. People were saying things like, "Oh, did you see the new Destiny's Child? They replaced two girls! Watch the video and see if you can pick out the new recruits." It was like a game for people to play.

You're Perfect—Now Change

Let me explain a little bit how the music industry works: We got a record deal. First, the label told me, "Congratulations!" The next thing said was, "We really need to work on your look." I had to undergo not a makeover, but a complete transformation. They made me cut my hair and lose weight. They totally criticized me and said, "Okay, Beyoncé, you need a new haircut. You need to get some more highlights, too. And you need to wear green all the time, because that's the color that complements your eyes. You also need to go on a diet. And start doing some sit-ups! You need to build up your calves as well. And I think we're going to style you like an . . . eighties chick. So, from this moment on, you will wear only green, eighties-style clothing." Whatever image they come up with, that's basically how it works.

So, yes, it's true. When Farrah later complained in an interview that we asked her to dye her hair, it was true. We needed one girl with red hair and one girl with black hair, because that's how the two girls who left looked. And that was also my mama's original vision for the group.

She dyed each of our hair a different color. We figured this way every fan could relate to at least one of us, and each of us would have her own distinctive look. And at the time Farrah was fine with it. "Okay," she said. "No big deal." It was a temporary cosmetic adjustment she had to make—and honestly, that's nothing. What's the big deal? It's just hair. That's when the media picked up on it and—as with many things—tried to turn it into a scandal.

Perhaps to some people outside of the music industry, having to dye your hair when you get into a band seems like a terrible thing, but they don't understand how this industry operates.

So to all the people who thought we were terrible for asking Farrah to color her hair for a few months, guess what? That was nothing at all. I mean, that's what happens in this business. She should consider herself very blessed that it's all she had to do, because Kelly and I had to do much more. I had to bleach my hair blond! My hair was so long and healthy—it was virgin hair. It didn't have any color on it. After dyeing it and bleaching it so much, I had to wear braids to give my hair a break because it broke off in the front. (And now I don't wear my real hair unless I'm doing a L'Oréal ad. I keep it braided up and protected, but that's not fun.) I can't blame anyone for that. It was my choice. I chose to be in the industry. Anyone who chooses to work in this industry will have to make sacrifices. We had to move away from our families. We used to jog every morning for miles, and then sing and rehearse dance routines all day, every day. Most kids live on Pop-Tarts and Kool-Aid—I was eating nothing but Lean Cuisine and soup. People think we are lying around the swimming pool, sunning ourselves, eating chocolate-covered strawberries and sipping Cristal—Crystal Lite is more like it!

NEGATIVE TO POSITIVE

I don't think some people like that we are young women who are successful and, on top of that, positive—that combination must seem intimidating. I think it's healthy for fans to know that we're not flawless. We make some mistakes—we're human. It's important to us that they know we're strong, but they also need to know we cry. We're hardly untouchable, and when someone says something mean, it hurts. But the wonderful thing about us is that we always learn from our mistakes—we find a way to turn it around and make it work to our advantage.

I have always been a huge fan of Madonna, and she is the best at making things work to her advantage. Madonna is much more than a singer, songwriter, and dancer—she is a mastermind of the music business. She's unstoppable. Every obstacle ever placed in her path, she's picked up and run with it—all the way to the bank. MTV banned her video? Okay—she sold it! If anybody said something bad about her—like when the press found out about her posing for nude pictures—her response was something like, "Yeah, I did. *And?*" It's one of the reasons she has been so successful. She's turned all the negative things into positive things. And that's what I try to do. (For the record, though, I would never pose nude.)

A Perfect Fit

When Kelly and I were holding auditions for new members, the first thing that I noticed about Michelle was her positive attitude. Michelle was willing to fly all the way down to Houston to try out for the group, so that right there told us she was serious. When she walked into our living room, Kelly and I were sitting next to each other on the couch, and we just looked at each other. We were thinking the same thing: She's the one! We could tell instantly.

Michelle has a real presence, and we could feel it even though she was standing in front of my coffee table and not on a stage. Most important, we knew she could sing, because she had already been around the world singing with Monica.

But the second we heard her voice, I breathed a sigh of relief and thought, Lord, thank you! This was the girl who we'd been looking for all our lives. She was eager and willing to work hard, which was more important to us than finding a girl who could move like Janet Jackson.

When Michelle joined the group, she really couldn't dance all that well—she'll be the first one to tell you that. We started teaching her routines, and at times she would get frustrated, but she still wanted to get it right. She wanted to stay in rehearsals until she had the moves down perfectly. Because of that drive, she caught on very fast, and we liked that. Through it all, she had such a great attitude—I never heard her complain once.

KELLY Michelle surprised us with her enthusiasm. Most people would have given up or whined about the long hours and the tough workouts. She's a doer, not a complainer, and that's what Beyoncé and I were looking for. In all our rehearsals she was open to constructive criticism—in fact, she encouraged it. She'd ask, "Did I do that kick okay? Was it high enough?" She may have had to try over and over again, but eventually she got it right. She knew that she could do whatever she set her mind to.

MICHELLE My rule to live by has always been: I don't care what it is you do—I love you. And if you're nice as well, then I love you even more. I loved Beyoncé and Kelly from the moment I first met them. I was on tour with Monica in July 1999. We were all taping a special for Nickelodeon in Sacramento, and Monica was the headlining act. Destiny's Child was opening for her, so we had a chance to chat during sound check. I saw the ladies again in Atlanta in November, because after the Monica tour ended, I had moved there hoping to pursue a singing career of my own. I said, "I don't know if you all remember me, I sang background for Monica . . ." And they said, "Yeah, of course!" They were so cool and down-to-earth. But I didn't walk away thinking that I would ever end up singing with them.

Then, in January 2000, I got a phone call from Destiny's Child's choreographer, Junella Segura. She had once danced for Monica, so we knew each other. That tour truly showed me who the angels of *mine* were—and Junella was most definitely one. For her to suggest my name to Beyoncé and Kelly surprised me, because we didn't really know each other all that well. It's not like Junella and I hung out a lot when we were on the road with Monica. We didn't get off tour and call each other every day, saying, "Hey, girl! What's up with you?" So for her to recommend me as a replacement for LaTavia and LeToya was really cool of her to do.

When she called me she said, "You know, Michelle, you were just so sweet and humble and nice to everybody, and you have a voice." I was speechless. I later made sure to thank her in my *Survivor* CD credits. I wrote: "You have truly helped in making my dream come true!! I thank you from the bottom of my heart, love you!!" She deserves the best. Something great is going to be there for her one day!

Imaging

When I was growing up in Rockford, I never dressed up—especially not in dresses. I never liked my legs. My prom dress was very demure—it was a long white satin dress with a V neck, and it didn't show much. The back may have been a low V cut, but I had a scarf around my neck and a long white train. So when I joined Destiny's Child, my mother was nervous that it would change me.

I knew for a fact that Mom would trip when she saw me on TV. And I was right. What happened was, after the "Destiny's Child boot camp"—getting down all the songs and the routines, which for me basically meant learning how to dance—I lost weight. Everywhere but my boobs, that is. And because I shed pounds from the other parts of my body, my boobs looked bigger than usual. My mother thought I was trying to be sexy, I guess. She was also scared, because she didn't know anything about the other singers or the management. She had no idea what my image was going to be like. But that was before she had met Miss Tina.

Miss Tina would never put me in anything that looked sleazy. When my mom got a chance to know Miss Tina and the rest of the Knowles family, she realized that Tina is a mom, too, and she protects her children. Once my mom understood that, she was cool. She's fine with the way I dress.

Tina is wonderful; she's helped me out so much—especially with my style. She helped me to discover another side of my personality. She always makes sure that I look nice. Like when I started wearing makeup for the first time. I had never worn makeup before—let alone gotten the very painful "facial hair removal" that I needed—but after I had the makeup artists work with me, I was like, "Oh, I don't look too bad with makeup on." That progressed to "I don't look too bad with my midriff showing." All my life I've been shy about certain things. I was shy about dancing. When I joined the group, I was expected to dance—in stiletto boots. I wondered, How come I can't be like Whitney Houston and just look pretty while I'm singing? She only dances every once in a while. But today's divas don't have it so easy. They have got to work much harder for the money. So I learned how to do it all. And I never could have done it without the support of Miss Tina and the group.

THREE FOR THE ROAD

11

BEYONCÉ Farrah was very quiet around the rest of us. Michelle, Kelly, and I would be singing, but we could sense her holding back. Basically, to make it short, she didn't fit in and everybody saw that—from people who didn't know us, to the people at the record label, to the fans. She is not a bad person; we just didn't click, and that's all.

Musically, her voice didn't blend in with ours, and I think that was her main concern. One time we were scheduled to perform on BET and we wanted to sing a number that had four lines and then a harmony part. We wanted each of us to have a line, and then at the end sing the harmony together. I was trying to figure out a way to make it work and to make Farrah comfortable, like changing the melody to make it fit one less voice or combining another voice with hers. In the end, we decided that we should all just harmonize with Farrah on her line.

Can We Talk?

In any organization, people try to fix problems before they grow into serious issues, because then it's easier to avoid an argument later on. In the early days of Destiny's Child, we didn't talk enough. I never wanted to start any problems, so I tried to ignore the fact that there were ongoing problems in the group. I wanted it to seem like everything was okay. Kelly was very passive, and she let the other members kind of run over her. Basically, we just let so much bad stuff fly without doing anything about it. And then it was too late.

So we learned from that experience and decided that in the future we would nip any little problems in the bud—just talk about them like adults who want a business to run smoothly. Kelly and I promised each other that if there was an incident or even a dirty look, we wouldn't scream and say, "Girl, why you lookin' at me like that?" Instead, we would step aside and talk to the person and say, "I'm sorry. I might be trippin', but I just want to talk to you because I was concerned about the look you gave me. Did it mean anything? If so, let's talk about it and fix the problem if there is one."

Before the incident in Seattle, we had many meetings with Farrah. Kelly and I would call meetings with the hope that it would be an opportunity for Farrah and Michelle to give input and feedback. It would be just the four of us in those meetings—I know it was rumored that my mom, dad, and sister would also sit in, but it's not true. It was just Kelly, Farrah, and Michelle, and I'd say, "If there's anything anyone doesn't like, please speak up." And no one ever did, so we were not aware of any problems. It was always little things that we would talk about.

My main concern was the fact that Farrah kept to herself. She was always sitting off to the side during interviews and she didn't seem enthusiastic about participating in our public appearances. When we would go out, she made some excuse why she couldn't come, or she would go out to events by herself and wouldn't even invite us. When trying to bond with a group in a short amount of time, that doesn't help.

There were other things, but nothing really deep. It just seemed like Farrah didn't really want to be in a group. I think she wanted to be on her own. I don't think her intention was to be in Destiny's Child for a long period of time.

And after she left us to our own devices in Seattle, it was pretty clear that she wanted nothing more to do with us. But despite that, I tried my best to convince her to come to Sydney and patch things up. Unfortunately, she said no. And we had no choice but to consider letting her go.

Kelly, Michelle, and I were scared. We couldn't imagine going through more drama after having just gone through it with the media over the rift with LeToya and LaTavia. We were just starting to get love from people, and now we were forced to risk it all again. It was the hardest decision we had to make, and it was terrifying. But God was with us, and that night in Sydney it was too peaceful and too perfect on the stage as a trio to ignore.

Walking on Sunshine

KELLY I hate to sound like a B-word, but the best feeling in the world was when we first appeared as a trio. Honestly, I felt a whole lot better once it was just us, simply because it felt like freedom. Yes, indeed, because I remember how intimidated I felt when the others were around. I felt insecure around them, like I wasn't talented when really I was. Without them, I had to grow so much more vocally. I needed to make up for the missing members. Before that, I felt uneasy. They made me feel shy, and now I realize that I was letting that hold me back.

Whenever I would finally try to come out of my shell, something would happen, a fight or a look, and I would crawl right back in. Australia was the first time I did not have to hold back one bit, because I knew there were two people on either side of me who loved me, and they would always be there for me. We didn't have to put on any kind of an act for one another—the love was for real. I didn't have to hide my feelings or be hyperconscious about unintentionally stepping on anybody's toes, because Beyoncé and Michelle understood me. I used to always feel like I was walking on eggshells—with everything I said and everything I did. And suddenly, there I was, walking on sunshine!

No Worries

Beyoncé, Michelle, and I were better than ever at that performance in Australia. The dynamic didn't change that dramatically. In fact, onstage we turned the act up a couple of notches, because we didn't want people walking out of there saying, "Oh, well, since they have one less member now, they just weren't as tight." No, we refused to let anyone think that. Our vocals were even better because Michelle is a great singer, and she sang her heart out that night. She really has a voice, and with Farrah gone, she had an opportunity to step out and show it.

I remember we called Mathew. He had been trying to calm our nerves before the performance by saying not to worry, everything was going to work out. He said once we stepped out on that stage, everything would seem just like the way it always was, and nothing would go wrong. Well, he was right again. We may have been a bit less sure of ourselves, but we said to Mathew, "Okay, if you say so." Once we finished the encore, we were like, "We can do this. This is easy. This is beautiful. This is perfect."

Early Warning Signs

MICHELLE I kind of always knew that Farrah would leave the group. I probably knew before Beyoncé and Kelly, because we were roommates while on the road. We'd share one room, and Beyoncé and Kelly would share the other. Farrah and I were getting close because we were both new members, and so we were each other's support system. The way she left was just so unfortunate, because I kept trying to talk her out of it. I would say, "Gosh, Farrah, whatever problems we might have, surely they can be worked out."

But Farrah could not let her concerns go—like the amount of time on camera. She'd say things like, "How come they show Beyoncé more?" And I'd say, "She's the lead singer. So why, when Beyoncé is singing lead, would they want to show us in the background doing nothing?"

She also disliked the long hours. And if you are working long hours with people you don't like, then the hours will seem even longer, because you have to sit around with people you despise. At first she acted like she wanted to be friends with us, but then when she finally got in the group, she was not happy.

Farrah let everyone know how unhappy she was—even MTV. Mathew had called her at her home in L.A. and told her that MTV wanted to tape an interview with all of us together at the Knowleses' house, and he asked her to fly to Houston. Farrah wanted MTV to fly to L.A. to tape her there. She could not understand that MTV already had their story line. The producers had already decided where they wanted to film us.

Farrah did fly to Houston, but when she walked in the door she was crying. I said, "Farrah, what is wrong with you, girl?" In between sobs, she said something like, "I was sick"—she had her hospital band on her wrist, as proof I suppose—"and even though I wasn't feeling well, Mathew told me I still had to come home to Houston."

She barely made it through our MTV taping, what with all that hysterical crying. And when the interview happened, she sat off to the side, apart from the rest of us. I remember her first words when she walked into the room were that she wasn't going to speak to Mathew. She knew what she was going to pull the minute she got out of the car. She acted like she didn't have any manners. She refused to even greet anyone. I don't care if she did have an argument with them the night before, she still should show respect and say, "Good morning. How you doing?" I asked her how she could act so ugly, and she said something like, "Well, I'm not going to speak to him because of something he said to me. He was mean." And I said, "Okay, girl, you must be trippin'."

Then I heard Mathew's side of the story, which was much more logical. It made sense. He said, "If she was really sick, why didn't she call earlier in the day?" It was unprofessional. As it turns out, Farrah wasn't admitted to the hospital. She went to the emergency room instead of a doctor because she didn't feel well. There is a big difference between dropping by the emergency room and actually being admitted to the hospital.

It would have been better if Farrah had leveled with us—she should have said, "Look, I don't agree with the group's decisions, and I can't handle it." But instead, she went on TV and insisted she was sick.

Anyone else would have called in advance, but Farrah made it harder for us, and then claimed that she was suffering from stress. She could not possibly have had any more stress than what we were going through because of her! But for the sake of the fans, we still knew we had to work and keep going.

Sayin' Good-Bye

When we were in Seattle, Farrah knew we had an important week of promotional work—hard work—ahead of us, and she was not looking forward to it. We had a meeting to discuss the problems she was having, but she ended up getting very upset. So she got up and left. I was sitting there with Beyoncé and Kelly, and figuring I know Farrah pretty well, I told them, "Look, I'm sure she just went out to get a breath of fresh air, but she'll be back." But she never came back. Ever. That was the last time I saw her.

After she left the meeting she went to our hotel room, got her stuff, made some flight arrangements, and returned to L.A. She left me a letter that said something like: "Michelle, I'm so sorry, but you know how I've been feeling." And yes, I knew she had been upset. She had every opportunity in meetings to say what was on her mind, but instead, she just abandoned us without saying a word, except for that letter. It made me so sad. I was like, Man, now what am I going to do? I didn't know if they were going to dissolve the group after that. Maybe the record company would decide we had way too many problems and they would refuse to put any more money behind us. At that point, I was worried this would be the end of Destiny's Child for good.

So I told Beyoncé and Kelly that I didn't want to go home. And they said, "Michelle, you don't have anything to worry about, because you didn't do anything. Farrah is the one who left." We ended up doing the Seattle radio show without Farrah, and we weren't prepared for that. It was a half-hour show. We were a bit nervous because people kept asking, "Where's Farrah?" We had to lie and say Farrah couldn't be there because she was sick. Later, MTV filmed us going to a seafood restaurant, and we ate on a deck overlooking the water. It was just the three of us and we had so much fun sitting down to dinner and acting goofy, even

BEYONCÉ: Independent women taking center stage on the *TRL* tour.

MICHELLE: On my birthday, with my doll birthday cake—the icing was her dress.

HELLY: I loved this red hat.

BEYONCÉ: Bootylicious at a young age. I don't think you're ready for this belly.

MICHELLE: Backstage before a photo shoot with photographer Mark Baptist for *InStyle* magazine's "Women Who Rock" issue.

BEYONCÉ: Striking a *Charlie's Angels* pose for the crowd at the Houston Rodeo. It was the largest crowd they ever had.

MICHELLE: A group hug with our manag[er] Mathew Knowles, before the 2000 Grammy Awards at L.A.'s Staples Center.

KELLY: Michelle, Beyoncé, our very talented stylist and designer Tina Knowles, Beyoncé's sister, Solange Knowles, and me backstage at the VH1/*Vogue* Fashion Awards.

KELLY: Cuddling with one of our youngest fans, Rebecca Morales, the daughter of our sound engineer, Ramon Morales.

MICHELLE: Hangin' with the troops—camo-coordinated—in Houston before an autograph signing for *Survivor*.

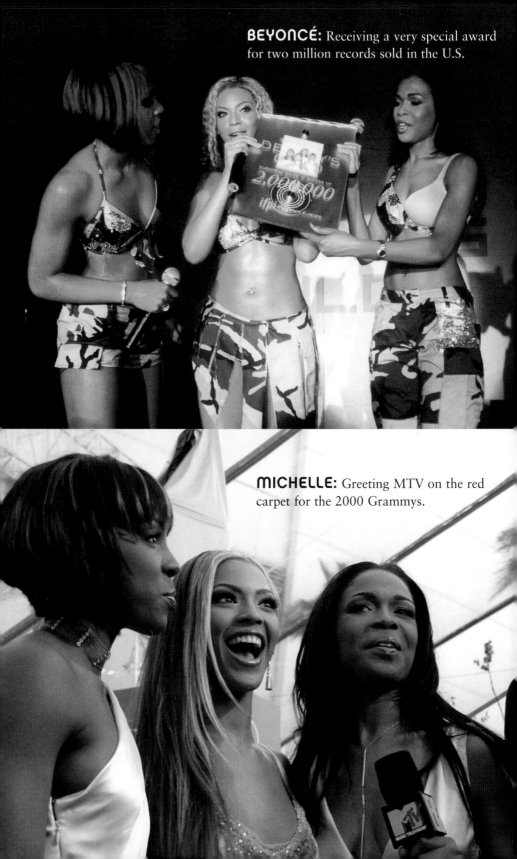

BEYONCÉ: Receiving a very special award for two million records sold in the U.S.

MICHELLE: Greeting MTV on the red carpet for the 2000 Grammys.

KELLY: Taping the "Say My Name" video. It was our first time performing with Michelle, and she did great.

BEYONCÉ: Taking a short break with the talented Rodney Jerkins, who produced "Say My Name."

BEYONCÉ: I love to wear hats, and I thought this was perfect for rehearsing at the Houston Rodeo.

KELLY: If my dog, Mohawk, saw this, he would be jealous, but I can't help it, I love dogs—even if they're not mine.

MICHELLE: On the *TRL* tour I had a chance to sing the classic "Ooh Child." It's a beautiful song.

KELLY: On the *TRL* tour, singing with soul. I've come a long way since I first started singing with Beyoncé.

BEYONCÉ: Music is such an emotional art form. It's how I express myself.

MICHELLE: My first photo shoot on the set of the "Say My Name" video.

KELLY: Breakin' it down on the *TRL* tour. It's hard to believe that in the early days I couldn't dance.

BEYONCÉ: Putting on a "Happy Face" on tour.

MICHELLE: Can you handle this?
Stylin' in our beautiful Grammy dresses,
which Tina, working with Versace, designed.

though we knew Farrah was gone. But we had to put that out of our minds for the moment.

The next morning I talked to Farrah. I called and tried to talk some sense into her. I said, "Farrah, you have got to remember that you walked into something that's already been established, so you just have to get used to it. Maybe when you get some seniority, that's when you could put your two cents in. You knew when you joined the group that Beyoncé was already the lead singer. So get over it."

I also reminded her that Kelly didn't join the group yesterday—she has always been there, for more than ten years. I said, "Look, I'm not going to walk into your house and, if you've had a picture in your living room for ten years—even if I didn't like it—I'm not going to move it and put it in the bathroom. If that's the way you want the picture, then okay, that's the way it's going to be. Beyoncé and Kelly have been doing this for years, and whatever they've been doing has been very successful. For the good of the group, you should let it go."

But she was adamant. She was saying things like, "No, I'm not going to Australia. I'll see you when y'all get back." So she was going to make us go by ourselves *and* do all the work. I told Farrah, "You think we're going to do all that work for you, come back, and then you can just go with the flow? It doesn't work like that because you did not leave correctly."

We tried talking Farrah into coming to Australia while we were waiting at LAX, but she kept saying she was too tired. She started raising her voice to Beyoncé, and Beyoncé is the type of person who, even if you raise your voice, she'll keep calm. I'm sure some of our dancers heard what was going on, but they didn't ask any questions about what happened. Later, Farrah tried to say that she never got our phone messages asking her to catch a later flight.

When there was no sign of Farrah in Sydney, Beyoncé, Kelly, and I finally accepted the fact that she would not be joining us. I was most afraid because Destiny's Child was kind of restarting, and the public had finally seemed to be accepting Farrah and me as the two new members. I was so worried because now we were going to have to go through some more drama. We really couldn't make a final decision about Farrah until we got back from Australia, even though we had made several international phone calls to Mathew. Things couldn't be properly settled until we got back home. But first we had to get through our press trip—as a trio.

ON MY OWN

Farrah and I had always shared the spotlight, since we were the two new members. So at that performance in Sydney, I felt like I really had something to prove. Onstage I could feel more eyes on me, because everyone was suddenly focusing on me. In some ways that was empowering, because I felt like I had more responsibility. And down deep, I wanted people to see me work. There were certain songs like "Killing Time" where the background vocals are so powerful that I almost had to sing them as lead vocals. When it came time to sing the a cappella gospel medley, I knew it was my moment to shine. It was my time now to prove why I'm in the group—because I can sing!

We did lots of interviews. We had some photo shoots, too. Whenever we go overseas, we work a lot because we want to do enough to last a few months. Sometimes we would do fifteen interviews in one day. Since Farrah wasn't there, it was an opportunity for me to talk more and answer some questions. But it wasn't all work.

Australia was a real bonding experience. We went to a pet sanctuary, because Kelly wanted to see the kangaroos and koala bears. We dropped by this little café and had hot cocoa and some bread and butter, because we love bread with butter. We had so much fun with our Australian rep. She took us shopping, because I forgot some underwear and shoes. I bought black boots while Angie, our assistant, went looking for underwear for me. It was funny, because the only underwear she could find had the days of the week written on them! Not only that, but they also glowed in the dark! After that we went to Burger King to experience what the Aussie burger was like.

Overall, Farrah is a nice person, but once she joined the group, she realized that she just couldn't live the type of life that she normally would live. Our lifestyle wasn't working for her. She should have just said, "I'm sorry, but I can't handle all the pressure and change. I thought I could but I was wrong."

Farrah actually called me not too long ago. It was when we were at the Houston airport getting ready to board a flight. I answered my phone and she started rehashing the same old story. As far as I'm concerned, that's ancient history. After all, I hadn't done anything, and I don't want to let anything coax me into negative thinking. So I haven't seen, talked to, or heard from her since.

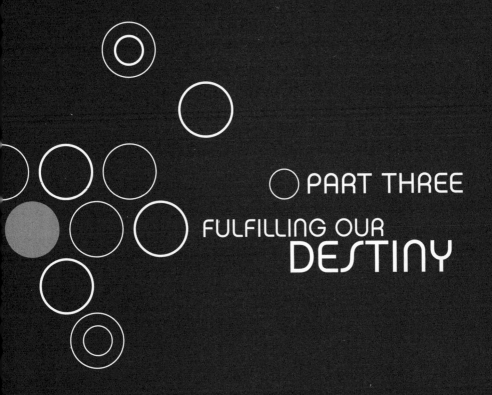

PART THREE

FULFILLING OUR
DESTINY

Our destiny exercises its influence over us even
when, as yet, we have not learned its nature: it is our
future that lays down the law of our today.

—Nietzsche

SURVIVORS 12

BEYONCÉ The plane ride back to Houston from Sydney seemed like it was much longer than seventeen hours, but at least it gave me plenty of time to think. As soon as we landed (and our jet lag wore off), Kelly, Michelle, and I sat down for a meeting with my father about the Farrah situation. We explained to him that after getting through the concert and endless promotional tour in Sydney as a trio—on our own—we realized that we could survive anything together. The three-day video shoot for the *Charlie's Angels* movie was only a few weeks away. We worked out all the legal details with Farrah, and in the end, it was an amicable split, a real win-win situation, so to speak. Well, at least until the media found out about it—the papers weren't about to report it that way. Let's just say that when the news hit, it really hit the fan.

I remember we called up *TRL*—we had to break the news about Farrah. So Carson Daly was the first person we told. And then we did some more interviews. It was tough for us because we felt like we had just been in this situation, and there we were once again, only a couple of months later. We were already scheduled to go on tour with Christina

Aguilera for about three months. Then when we came back we started recording the new record.

At any rate, the stories in the media provided me with a lot of inspiration. We wanted to get a new CD out as soon as possible, so that it would coincide with the release of the film, and personally, I couldn't wait to get back into the recording studio. I wanted to write lyrics that expressed everything Kelly, Michelle, and I had been through together—the high notes, the low notes, and, most important, how through our persevering spirits we eventually found perfect harmony. But still, whenever I would finish a song, I had to hum the melody and speak the words real softly. And they would say, "Come on, B. Belt out that song!" And then I would try to sing it a little louder.

Survivor—the Album

Music is such an emotional art form. Perhaps that's why I was very self-conscious when crafting the tracks for *Survivor*. Thank goodness I had Kelly and Michelle there with me; they help me through everything.

"HAPPY FACE"

They inspired me to write "Happy Face." In the song I say there are plenty of people who don't like me, but there are ten times more who love me, and aside from that, I love myself. The song talks about waking up to the sun shining and outside is a beautiful day. The night before I wrote that I was sad and alone in my room, and suddenly the next day I thought, Why am I complaining? I'm so blessed. Even if I didn't ever make it in the music industry, I'm lucky just to be alive and healthy, to have my family, and to have friends like Kelly and Michelle. I'm blessed. I used to dream about achieving this level of success. I have to put on a happy face. There are so many people out there who want to be in my shoes—of course, they don't realize that my shoes are uncomfortable and they give me blisters—but I can't complain. People think I live in an MTV Barbie World, but I don't. There's no pink Corvette in my driveway, and there's no perfect Ken to help make my life less lonely. I am by no means a living doll.

"SURVIVOR"

The most rewarding aspect is getting to touch so many lives with my songs. "Survivor" has had a great impact on people. I've seen kids in the audience in wheelchairs with the biggest smiles on their faces while I'm singing it. I see the hope in their eyes—that song makes them realize they have got a chance. I have met hundreds of children who are suffering from cancer and they always sing it to me—they may not have hair, but they have beautiful smiles—like they have nothing to complain about. They are so strong, and seeing them gives me strength. Those are some of the most special people, who I consider myself blessed to meet.

I have a radio DJ to thank for the inspiration for that song. When Farrah's departure was made public and the tabloids got a hold of the story, they had a field day. It was on the bus, while we were on tour with Christina Aguilera, that I heard some early morning DJ make a crack that being a member of Destiny's Child was just like being in the reality–TV show *Survivor*. At first I got so mad! To this day, I don't listen to morning radio shows. I can't. They make me cringe. I felt like screaming. But then I took a deep breath and thought, Okay, mister, I'll show you: I'm gonna take that nasty remark you made and turn it into something

positive. The following night we had to fly to the next city and I wrote the song on the plane. I wrote it quickly because I was so frustrated. The words just came pouring out. I wrote a song about what it really means to be a survivor.

"INDEPENDENT WOMEN"

Charlie's Angels was our first brush with Hollywood. I had written "Independent Women Part 1" before I even knew that Drew Barrymore had plans to make a movie of Charlie's Angels. It's cool how it all worked out. McG, the film's director, used to direct music videos, and he came down to the set of our video shoot to meet with us. Of course, I had no idea when I wrote it that it would be the first single from the Charlie's Angels soundtrack and that we would make a splashy video. I didn't even think that our label would be willing to spend the money to let us make a video. What a major production it turned out to be—three days of shooting, Versace outfits, and cameos by Drew, Cameron Diaz, and Lucy Liu! The song actually ended up in the *Guinness Book of World Records* as one of the biggest songs in history. It broke a bunch of records.

And not just in America, but all over the world. "Independent Women" is about working very hard and accomplishing what you want out of life and being able to provide for yourself. It salutes all of the women in the world who are single mothers—if they see a dress they like at the mall, they shouldn't have to depend on their boyfriends or their parents to get it for them. I'm not trying to say that you can't accept help from people if you need it, but you shouldn't constantly depend on other people to do things for you if you can help yourself. The song is not a celebration of material goods like flashy cars and big rocks, it's just celebrating women who work hard to get what they want.

"Independent Women Part 1" made a huge cultural impact in Japan. Until that song became a hit, young girls and teenagers there thought it wasn't cool to buy their own stuff. The thing to do was to get a boyfriend and have him buy everything. Then after "Independent Women" came out, all those girls were like, "You know what? I'm going to pay my own bills. I'm going to get my own phone. I'm going to buy my own jewelry." The youth culture changed—for the better, I think—all because of one song. A song I wrote. That just amazes me.

I was only nineteen years old when I penned that song. I feel so lucky. I used the phrase "Independent Women," because some people misunderstood "Bills, Bills, Bills," and they thought we were a bunch of gold diggers. I was like, Hey, we're not gold diggers; we're independent women! But some people only listened to part of the song, and formed an opinion about it based on that alone. It's like a book—you cannot read the first page and think you know how the story is going to end. You have to read the whole thing. The same goes for songs. You have to listen to all of the lyrics in the song because it tells a tale. "Bills, Bills, Bills" was about a guy who ran up our credit cards and took advantage of us, and we wanted to inspire people to get rid of bad guys who try to control them.

It seems that the songs I write because of extreme anger, happiness, or sadness become the biggest hits. I guess that's because a lot of other people can relate to them. For me the studio is where I go to get stuff off my chest and melodies out of my head. It's my therapy. I write down whatever I'm feeling, and then I sing it. Words are more powerful when I sing them than when I speak them.

A Dream Come True

MICHELLE Since I've joined the group, Beyoncé, Kelly, and I have had a ball together. I know all the things that those girls have been through, and for them to come out smiling and stronger, well, that gives me strength—knowing that I can make it through anything, too. So I really look up to them. They are some strong girls and they have got a lot of knowledge. For them to be doing what they have always wanted to do—for us to be able to walk into a store and get whatever we might want to get—that is a long-overdue reward.

●Our greatest love is performing, and to see them so excited inspires me. They are my sisters, just like my biological sisters, Danielle and Cameron. And I love all of my siblings equally. Beyoncé and Kelly hold a huge space in my heart. Mathew and Tina are like my parents now. Mathew hugs me and offers advice like a dad, and Tina and I do mother-daughter things. She even takes me shopping. We went together to get some pictures and furniture for my apartment—my own place.

I never thought that I would be doing anything like this. I recently looked at myself in the mirror, and I couldn't believe I had Reggie Wells doing my makeup. Reggie Wells is huge. He is Oprah Winfrey's personal makeup artist. He is a legend in his field. I have also had the pleasure of working with makeup artist Billy B. That is very cool to me. One day I will be retired from this and I can say, "You know, we worked with the best." It's great to work with people who you know love you, instead of working with somebody who is just working with you because it's their job. Definitely we have been blessed, and I continue to count our blessings.

My self-esteem has blossomed since we became a trio. I cannot believe that I have stood on a stage at the Grammys wearing short shorts in front of millions of people. That was a major achievement for me. I have never, ever worn shorts, because I have always hated my legs. Even when I was a little girl and it was hot outside, I still wore jeans. I always was more comfortable in pants and a tank top than in a sundress. My legs always seemed too skinny and scrawny, like two upside-down baseball bats—there was no definition or tone. As if that weren't bad enough, I also have these little black spots all over my knees.

It's funny that some people have this idea that we think we're perfect, because we all have things we hate about our bodies. We're human. I haven't completely overcome my body image hang-ups yet—I think that's a problem I share with a lot of women. But I have made great progress. I just try to remember that no one is perfect, everybody has flaws. Now I actually say to myself, "Okay, Michelle, only you know that you hate your legs and think they could be a lot more muscular." And as for the dark spots, I depend on a little trade secret. It's called makeup. I have learned to pick out and focus on my better qualities—that's the key. Miss Tina's beautiful costume visions have inspired me to do that. You

may think, I don't have very nice legs, but you definitely have something that's cute. Maybe you have nice arms or hands or a bootylicious butt. That is up to you to discover, but it is definitely there somewhere.

Holding My Own

KELLY With each and every new album I realize how we've continued to grow, especially with the release of *Survivor*. I can definitely say that where I am at now is not where I was when I started singing with Beyoncé about ten years ago. I've experienced a lot of personal growth, whether it was building up my confidence, voice lessons, or feeling that in terms of dancing, I can finally hold my own onstage.

When I first joined the group, I could not dance. Not at all. Honestly, I had the worst sense of rhythm. The girls would try to show me certain steps and they would say, "No, Kelly, the move goes like this," and I would stumble— my legs falling everywhere—and make them mess up. When they were moving to the right, I'd be going left. I was all jacked up. Finally, after countless rehearsals, I'd get it down. My mom would get sick of me then. I would come home late—we wouldn't finish rehearsals until about eight or nine o'clock—and I'd blast the music real loud and dance some more. Or sometimes I would stay over at Beyoncé's house, and her parents would be sitting in the living room waiting for us to finish doing a routine, saying, "Y'all need to do your homework." And we would plead with them, "Just give us ten minutes." So they would ask us again later and then we would ask for ten more minutes. Beyoncé was always trying to help me work on my steps.

Early on, when I was eleven, I took a couple of classes with Beyoncé's dance teacher, Miss Darlett. She was nice, but she was hard on all of us. When I was a kid, I was very sensitive. Everything people told me made me cry. I was just a little punk—anybody could make me cry. I was such a baby, and I should have just chilled out. Shedding all those tears didn't get me anywhere. Basically, I was a brat. But no matter how much I cried, Miss Darlett would never turn me away. She would just put her hand on my shoulder and try to comfort me. She was always trying to help me out. But I didn't stay with the lessons for long; instead I switched to voice lessons.

I started taking voice lessons when I was twelve, because Beyoncé told me she took them. I loved the way she could sing, so it didn't take long for me to sign up. I definitely believe in them. A lot of people think voice lessons teach you how to sing, but actually, they teach you how to sing correctly. You either have a voice or you don't! But to sing like Whitney Houston, you have got to work.

Some people—like Whitney, for example—were lucky enough to be born with an extraordinary gift, but most other singers have to train their voice. And in order to do that, you need to learn how to breathe right. You also need to learn how to put the notes in the proper parts of your vocal cords. It may sound weird, but it works.

My first vocal coach was named David Brewer. He always used to tell me that my voice was beautiful, because it was so clear. But when I was a kid, I didn't love it. I would hear somebody else's voice, and I wanted to sound like them. After all, your voice represents your beauty and your uniqueness. Honestly, though, I'm still learning how to improve it, and there's nothing wrong with that. I now embrace the fact that my voice is airy and angelic, and I'm happy that a lot of people like it.

I have gradually come to love dancing, too. When I first started out, my problem was that I had no confidence in myself. The ability to dance is definitely all in your head. You need to say to yourself, I am going to get this dance step down, because if you don't you will surely mess up. It's not nearly as hard for me to dance now as it used to be. I used to always get so discouraged with myself. For me it was just work—painful work, at that—and I just wanted to get the moves down so that I didn't have to do them any longer. I didn't like it as much as I like singing.

Singing has so much feeling—you can hear the pain in a voice. You can hear the soul. When you listen to artists like Marvin Gaye, Aretha Franklin, Chaka Khan, and Donny Hathaway, they have so much soul in their voices that you hear their joy or pain and you relate to it. Dance is not like that for me. There are a lot of incredible dancers who can do that with their bodies, but I think they must be double-jointed.

My motivation came from watching all the great dancers perform—mainly Janet Jackson. I love Janet. And I decided that if she can sing and dance and enjoy it, then I was going to do it, too. And I seriously made an effort. I saw how long and hard she worked and how she critiqued every single one of her moves●It was so amazing to me. Michael did that, too. The way he moonwalks is sick! Nobody can mock Michael. He cannot be touched at all.

It wasn't until the beginning of *The Writing's on the Wall* that dancing seemed more like fun. When I went into the studio with the choreographer, I eventually realized that if I tried to catch the dance steps when the instructor first showed them to me, then I did okay. And I noticed that when I did it the second time, I got a little bit better. The third time I almost had it, and the fourth time, bam! It was done. At first I couldn't do that, so I would get down on myself, thinking that I would never be able to dance like that. And guess what? When you tell yourself that you can't do something, you really can't. That's why I say it's really all in the mind.

I passed on this information to Michelle when she first joined the group, because I started to see myself in her all over again—she obviously hated dancing. I couldn't blame her, but I said, "Michelle, I'm going to let you in on a little secret, because I think that I used to feel exactly how you feel about dancing." And once I explained it to her, she started dancing much better. And she's a great dancer now.

Stage Presence

I think the great thing about Michelle, Beyoncé, and me is the fact that we know when to cut the diva mode off. How would I define a diva? It's a little bit of cockiness—showing you're not afraid. You have to exude strength and confidence. You have to show people that it's all about you when you're on that stage, like this is *my* stage. When we get onstage, we do our thing—we *work it*. But that doesn't carry *off* the stage. And that's exactly how we want it to be. Because when you take that attitude offstage, it becomes a problem. You start feeling like it's all about you, but it's not. It's about the people around you, like Mathew and Tina, who are working hard to make sure that you succeed. It's about God making all these plans for you.

I had to overcome my fear of performing by praying and asking God to give me strength and calm me down. There are still times that my voice gets shaky, and if I start to get the jitters inside that can disrupt my performance, it can mess up the sound bad.

Performing for the Pres

BEYONCÉ: I never thought that I would meet—let alone perform for—the president of our country.

MICHELLE: We performed at the presidential inauguration. It was our chance to reach out to the American people. I've never ever met a president before, so to meet President Bush and his wife was a great experience. (I think we gave their daughters two-way pagers as gifts.) He said it was kind of our duty and responsibility to hold up high standards and a good image, because so many people look up to us. He also said that he appreciates our music. It's good to know that the president of the United States is a fan.

KELLY: The performance was nothing political, which is what we like. We have our own opinions, and we don't want people to think exactly what we think in terms of politics. We just wanted to show up and be Destiny's Child. We performed, and it was a benefit for kids—they had a lot of fun.

The president was very down-to-earth. He was talking to us, and he said something like, "You know, you guys really are blessed to be in the situation that you are in—you can reach people that I can't reach. And I just love the way you are so positive and y'all got a great image." He was so cool. He had security people around him, but it wasn't real obvious. I loved that he was sitting around talking to us. After all, he's from Texas, too, so we could relate.

Trouble Shooting

BEYONCÉ I've learned from past mistakes that so many things can be totally misconstrued in the media. So when you're in a group, you have to try to avoid things that will look to the media like a problem, even though it isn't one. For instance, once, we were all in New York, and I had a photo shoot for the cover of *Vanity Fair*'s music issue. Kelly and Michelle had planned to leave for Houston the day before me, and I was going to stay a day later, because of the shoot. But then they decided to hang out in New York for an extra day. They had first-class seats, but because they changed their flights, the airline only had business-class seats left for the next day. I already had a first-class seat. But I had to worry, What if the flight attendants see me up in first class and the other girls back in business class? To them it might look like I always travel first class and make the others fly business. I didn't want that kind of rumor to get started—and I felt bad about sitting in first class, anyway—so I chose not to sit up there. I gave up my seat and we sat together in business class. I didn't have to do that. It wasn't a big deal to Kelly and Michelle. But still, I didn't want it to be a gossip item in some tabloid.

We've also learned to make sure we keep the lines of communication open. We have regular meetings. If somebody is feeling bad about something, we talk about it and help one another. When somebody is insecure or upset, we're sensitive about that. We try to solve it together, and we do help one another. For instance, if I'm trying to lose weight—and I am always trying to lose a little weight—and I go on one of those horrible no-bread, no-rice, no-pasta, low-carb diets, Kelly and Michelle won't eat pizza in front of me. I know that they eat—I know when they just had a hot fudge sundae or an apple pie à la mode! Thankfully, though, they eat all that stuff when I leave. If Kelly is trying to learn a song or she's in voice lessons, Michelle and I will stay out of the way and give her space. Those are just some of the ways that we support one another. When I do something that might seem self-promotional, it's really to benefit the whole group. For instance, me being on the cover of *Vanity Fair*: a lot of people who didn't know about us before that, they know about us now. It was my picture, but the caption said "Beyoncé Knowles of Destiny's Child."

We each seem to have our own individual fans. Somebody might not like me and like Kelly instead, because they feel like they relate to her more. I can't trip off that. I know it has to be hard for Michelle and Kelly, because they must get sick of people always making snippy little comments about me or us. I respect how well they handle it. It would be so easy to start hating on me when I get the attention, but they never do that. That's because they are secure in their talent—they have nothing to worry about.

We are proud to say that we have worked hard all our lives, and that paid off last year in the form of two Grammy Awards.

JUMPIN'
JUMPIN'

13

KELLY At the 2000 Grammy Awards I was a nervous wreck. Even though I found out that we had won our first award before we made it to the show! The Grammys had already started, and we were still at the hotel—as usual, we were running a little bit late. Beyoncé, Michelle, and I were going through our style checklist: Hair? Check. Makeup? Check. Outfits? Cute! Just then our publicist, Yvette Noel-Schure, burst into the room. I thought she came to hurry us along, but she had a huge smile on her face and she said, "Congratulations, Grammy Award winner Destiny's Child!" We had won for Best R&B Song. We all just started screaming and hugging one another. We all had on these very form-fitting Versace dresses, and we must have looked like colorful little pogo sticks jumping around the room. We were thrilled.

When the limo dropped us off on the red carpet in front of the Staples Center, we were all smiles—we definitely had something aside from our outfits to talk about. It's a great feeling to win an award before you even walk in the door. But our excitement quickly translated into nervous energy. We had to hurry backstage, because we were scheduled to

perform after Madonna sang "Music." She is a hard act to follow.

Everybody's hands were sweaty, and let me say something about my sister, Beyoncé—she is never worried or nervous about any performance, and if she is, she hides it away from Michelle and me. But that night, I could tell Beyoncé was nervous. Her palms were sweating so bad that when I grabbed her hand to pray, I was like, Ew! But I held tight, and we prayed. I could almost hear Michelle's legs shaking—she was shaking out of control, shivering like it was cold. And even though Beyoncé was clearly nervous, she led our prayer, and we were able to go into a peaceful zone and focus. When we heard the introductory notes of the song, each one of us took a deep breath. We released our hands and the curtain slowly rose.

I think the audience could sense that we were worried. The first thing I saw was Madonna sitting in the front row staring at us. She had a skeptical look on her face. Honestly, to have a huge superstar like her looking at us—that made me nervous as crap. But five minutes later, when our medley was over, everyone in the audience was on their feet applauding. So many people came up to us after the show to compliment us—legends like Elton John and Dolly Parton. Dolly told us, "Way to go, girls!" Then the CEO and chairman of Sony Music, Tommy Mottola, ran backstage and said, "All right, girls!" He was so excited for us; everybody was. It felt like it was our night.

Later on people kept raising toasts to us. (We couldn't toast back because we don't drink, but we appreciated the gesture.) We had pictures taken with everybody. I have always dreamed of winning a Grammy. And when I finally got one, I was shocked. The experience changed us, but for the better. It made all of us want to work even harder, because we want more Grammys!

I know that someday Beyoncé will get a Grammy for songwriting. She was nominated for one that night for writing "Independent Women Part 1." I kept saying, "Oh, Beyoncé, it's yours. That trophy belongs to you." I was so excited for her. And I remember that when she lost, she took it very well. "Oh, well, maybe next year," she said. I was upset, but not mad. I think she should have gotten that award. She's had it in for music since she was a baby. She's been producing our vocal arrangements since we were nine years old. Even then she knew this part should go with this part—she knew how to blend vocals and everything. She was always brilliant. What can I say? I give credit when credit is due.

But we had plenty of things to be happy about. When I was backstage, my best friend called me to say, "Do you know that Bono just came on TV and said that he's a Destiny's Child fan?" I could not believe it. We usually go home to bed, but after the Grammys, we had to celebrate. We went to Sony's party at a nice restaurant called Ago. Elton John and Tony Bennett were in the house! The room was full of all these incredible artists and major record execs. We realized that we were in the midst of all these cool people who have won Grammys, and now we had one, too— actually, we had two. We belonged to the club. We were trophy-carrying members. It was a great feeling.

The Performance

MICHELLE Next to the concert in Sydney, the Grammys may have been our strongest performance. It was the opportunity to redeem ourselves.

In order to get asked to perform at the Grammys, you have to have a certain amount of clout. When Recording Academy President and CEO Michael Greene is on the phone inviting you to rock the house, that's something.

I couldn't look at anybody. I was more nervous than excited—this was the Grammys. I was worried. I had to walk down a flight of steps—in stilettos. I knew the routine had to be tight. I couldn't mess up at the Grammys. There are some shows where if I mess up, I can correct it—I'll just sing a little harder or louder and overpower the mistake I made. But the Grammys performance was live. And live shows sometimes scare me.

Backstage, my legs were shaking. We were all shaking. Beyoncé and Kelly were wearing turquoise sequined dresses, but my outfit was special. I had on pants for the first part of the performance when we came down the steps. They were lined with Velcro down the side, so that when I did my costume change, all I had to do was pull the legs off and they transformed into shorts. It was supposed to be simple.

I only had a matter of seconds to change backstage, but when I got there my pant leg got caught on my boot. The song started and I was supposed to walk out onstage, but my pants were stuck. I missed my cue, which was my favorite part of the routine. It was so embarrassing. I was backstage saying, "I can't go out there now. I am not going to go out there now. I'm too late. I missed my cue—my favorite part— the moment we were supposed to toss off our hats into the audience." I thought, Beyoncé and Kelly will just have to finish the song without me.

I was worried that with three of us, if I came out too late it would look like a mistake. If four of us had been there, then two could have come out in the beginning, and then two more could come out later. Then it might have seemed intentional. And it would have been different if Kelly and I were already out there and then Beyoncé joined us, because she sings lead. If her outfit had gotten stuck, she could just come out and act like that was supposed to happen. But with Beyoncé and Kelly already out there, I felt like once I missed my cue, it was the point of no return.

Backstage Miss Tina was saying, "Michelle, you have got to go out there." She grabbed my hand. "Go. You can do it." And I thought about it—for about a second. It was the Grammys. We were live on national TV. Luckily, Miss

Tina was there. Talk about a fashion emergency. Somehow she snapped off that outfit. I don't know how she got it off me, but all that mattered is that it was off.

I found the nerve to get out there. I started doing the slow walk that we had rehearsed, but then I realized: If I keep walking this slowly, the song will be over by the time I make it over to Beyoncé and Kelly. I had to take bigger steps. We didn't prepare for anything like this in rehearsal. I had to think on my feet. On my stilettos!

The good thing is that nobody caught on. We were the only ones who knew about the mistake, and we decided not to tell anybody about it. I don't even know what happened but no more Velcro for me! Still, everybody stood up and clapped for us. Finally, we were met with industry approval.

I didn't look in the audience at all during the performance. Well, I may have peeked. I did see some people I knew, like producers Jimmy Jam and Terry Lewis. They're real cool, and they've always been sweet to me. I saw them out there in the audience smiling, nodding their heads, and clapping. But I wasn't looking for anyone—I knew the place where Madonna and people like that would be sitting, and I wouldn't even let myself look in that direction.

Afterward, there were so many parties. Beyoncé, Kelly, and I went to three in one night, and it was congratulations all around. Sir Elton John gave us a hug and a kiss, and he invited us to another party! Jill Scott was there and she was really, really cool. And Lil Bow Wow—he was too cute. He is on his way to becoming a man, but still too young for me.

Rockin' the House

BEYONCÉ We were nominated for "Say My Name," so of course the producer of the Grammys wanted us to perform that song. But "Independent Women Part I" was our current hit single, so we wanted to put some of that in the performance, too. It was the number one song in the country at the time. So we compromised by singing a medley of both songs.

Out of any performance, I can say that night was the most nervous I have ever been in my life. We had been nominated for five awards, and we felt that everybody was wondering, Okay, why are these girls up for so many Grammys? They wanted to see if we were for real. I'll never forget all of the people in the audience who were shooting us skeptical looks in the very beginning—they were like, What do y'all think you're doing up on that stage? But by the end of the performance, everybody was on their feet clapping. The Staples Center was one big standing ovation when we walked back to take our seats.

It could have been a disaster. When we first started walking down the steps to the stage, looking out at the sea of faces, it was the scariest feeling in the world. Then, when I thought the ache in my stomach couldn't get any worse, I saw Madonna sitting there, right in front of the stage. And as I walked down the staircase, I clutched the railing for dear life, and I kept thinking, Oh my God, there's Madonna! What am I doing here? What are we doing?

It was our first time performing as a trio on a big, big show. We had to do a good job, because we had something to prove. Plus, my mom wanted us to look glamorous, so she convinced us to wear stilettos—walking down a spiral staircase in them is about as easy as crossing a tightrope. On top of that, we had to sing and remember our choreography, and we only had two days to rehearse the routine, usually two hours a day at the most. We also planned to do a quick change during the show—so if something went wrong, we would be stuck. Worse than that—ruined. Suffice it to say, there was a lot of pressure on our backs.

The second before we started, we grabbed our microphones and took our positions on the stage as the lights were about to come up. We held hands for a quick prayer and then this sense of peace washed over us. "Ladies, get ready to show the Grammys what we are all about," I said. And when we let go of one another's hands, I was calm. A loud voice announced, "Destiny's Child," the music kicked in, and we did our thing. We remembered all of the steps and we rocked the house! Granted, Michelle's outfit change almost didn't happen, but she still made it out there. We finished the song and it was fierce. Are we survivors or what?

I could see that people were standing up and the clapping sounded like thunder. I was so happy. And then right after that, we won another award! This time it was for Best R&B Performance by a Duo or Group. Then we got even more love from the audience. We were practically in tears at the podium. We were overcome with joy. I didn't even have time to thank everyone—I needed to hurry backstage and find a box of Kleenex!

I was nominated for a Grammy as a songwriter, and that is huge. I was up against veterans who have written countless number one songs. These people are professional hit makers, not performers, and they are responsible for churning out love ballads for the Celine Dions of the world. I was the youngest person in that category. It was such a great honor for me, even though I didn't win. I was really thrilled to even be nominated. I still get shy about the songwriting process. It's something that I need to do in private. I can't write songs in front of people, because I get so self-conscious and flustered that I can't concentrate. But the Grammy nomination definitely helped to boost up my songwriting self-esteem a little bit.

Later that night at the Sony after-party, Sir Elton John gave each of us a kiss on the cheek and he told us congratulations. Earlier, Bono had given us a shout-out onstage, and that was amazing. Those two are icons—getting praise from them was almost better than winning the award. I also got a hug from the conga queen herself, Gloria Estefan. And I met Shakira that night, too. She's really cool—I noticed that we kind of look alike. I loved every minute of the party.

We keep our Grammys in the reflection room at home in Houston—we call it that because it contains all of our trophies and prizes. The walls are nearly covered with plaques from multiplatinum record sales. That's where Kelly also keeps her awards, so there are two of everything. We actually have four Grammys in there.

Keeping It Real

A few reviewers have suggested that our music isn't real music—apparently because it has commercial appeal—and we have often been dismissed as "just another pop group." Those critics have no idea what Destiny's Child is about. If you pull the plugs on our music, we can sing a cappella and bring the house down—even a house the size of the Staples Center. We have not been manufactured, and we didn't just roll off the assembly-line conveyer belt at any pop-music factory. I write our songs, not some producer who has never even met us. We come up with our own arrangements, and there is something powerful behind our songs—soul. The National Recording Academy is not going to nominate a group that's not writing real music. They wouldn't award them two Grammys.

R-E-S-P-E-C-T

Pop artists have a tough time getting respect, and regardless of the genre of music, once you sell over two million records, the industry considers you a pop artist. Which should be great, because it means everybody is buying your music and they like you. But it's a catch-22, because once you start doing really well, they don't like you anymore. They say, "She thinks she's all that now!" It's like when in the neighborhood some guy dreams of becoming a basketball star, so he is always playing at the local court. Everybody there is cool with him; they think he's down. Then he gets a chance to try out for a major team and he makes it. The same people who used to like him are now saying that he sold out. That's how it is in the music industry, too. Nelly Furtado has a great track on her album that basically says, "You like me until they play my song on the radio." That is so true.

Even though the music industry has always been youth-oriented, young artists aren't often treated with the same level of respect. As a female teenage R&B pop singer, there were so many stereotypes attached to me. I have had to confront—and conquer—them all. I may be young, but I am still old enough to realize exactly what I am up against. I know that a lot of people might write better songs and sing better than Destiny's Child. I've got a long way to go yet, but I am going to get there, and I am on my way. But at this point, we have definitely worked hard and achieved enough to get the respect we deserve. That's why it was really cool to hear someone of Bono's stature give us props at the 2000 Grammys. After that, I could care less what any reviewer thinks.

It's not just in the music industry that young people have problems getting respect. Young adults in general seem to have that problem. If I say, "My nerves are bad tonight," someone might respond, "Oh, you're too young to even have nerves." Or say some girl is in a funk because she and her boyfriend just broke up. Her parents might not think that she has a right to be sad. They'll say, "Aw, you're too young, little girl. You don't know anything about love." That's such a condescending attitude. When you're young, sadness hurts just as bad as it does when you get older. Your capacity for feeling doesn't change. Your emotions are real no matter what your age.

In any business environment young people have to work extra hard because the older, more experienced people there might not take them seriously, even if they are just as qualified. Some elders can't handle it when a youngster comes along and starts accomplishing the same tasks that they do—it catches them off guard and they are reluctant to give you respect. But there comes a time when you have to prove yourself, and once you do, they can't discredit you anymore.

HEROE*S*

BEYONCÉ We are truly blessed to have so many people who have inspired us along the way. People who have touched our lives both musically and personally. Some are people we looked up to growing up as kids—Michael Jackson, Whitney Houston, Shelia E.—and others are people who have been there for us day in and day out, pushing us to be our best. Without their influence we would not have been able to come this far.

Everyday Heroes

Teresa LaBarbera Whites is an amazing woman. She is the executive at Columbia Records who gave us our second chance. Teresa believed in us enough to fly us to New York to do a showcase. She became our A&R rep, which is a person who finds the best producers and musicians to work on records. She is also our very good friend. She's believed in us from the very beginning. I owe her a lot. She recognized our talent when we were only eleven. She is truly a wonderful lady.

KELLY Our vocal teacher, Kim Woods, is the best. Actually, she's more than just a voice coach— she's a dear friend and a fellow Christian. Whenever I'm feeling worried about a show, I can call her up and say, "Kim, I don't know about this performance. I'm scared." And the first thing she'll say is "Let's pray." Then I'll go and have a great show.

She understands the medical part of the voice. If I call her and I'm hoarse, she'll tell me, "Get off this phone right now. You've got to be quiet—you know that." Because she knows the medical side as well as the technical side, she can determine if I'm singing correctly. She'll give me advice like "Open the back of your throat and then put your tongue down." We have been working with her for four years now—since we started work on *The Writing's on the Wall*.

We work with her every other day: Monday, Wednesday, and Friday for thirty minutes to an hour. Thirty minutes is only when we are trying to get a lesson in; an hour is when we are trying to strengthen and improve our voices. My voice has changed dramatically. I can finally do stuff that I always wanted to do, like the incredible vocal runs I hear Whitney Houston do. The part I sing on the gospel medley— I could not have done that two years ago. We were amazed when we became able to hit those high notes. And still when we hit them, we'll look over at one another like, I did it!

Voice lessons teach you how to breathe correctly while singing. If you can hold a note for a long time, then you have to give thanks to voice lessons, because they teach you how to sing from your stomach. A lot of people don't realize that, and they sing from their throat. You're not supposed to do that, because if you do, you're not going to have any voice left at all. It causes polyps and nodules to grow on your vocal cords, and they'll stop you from singing freely. And that's the worst. Imagine not being able to use your voice for an entire year! Oh my gosh, I'd go ballistic. My two-way-pager bill would break me. I'm serious.

MICHELLE Kim is awesome. She has techniques! She's based in Nashville, but she travels back and forth to Houston, where her sister lives. We talk all the time: If I'm feeling hoarse, I'll call her before I go into the studio and she helps me open up my voice. When my voice is weak, she knows how to make it stronger. Not only is she our vocal coach, she's also a friend. She's a praying woman, very spiritual, and she always knows if something is wrong. When we're feeling down, she calls at just the right time or else two-ways us. She's the first professional vocal coach I've ever worked with. I always knew that the right vocal coach could take my voice and work wonders with it. Now I'm able to do things that I thought I could never do. At one point I even worried that I had lost my high range, but after working with Kim and doing her vocal exercises, I found that it was still there. She's always encouraging me to drink lots of water, too. I hate water! She and her husband, Ray, and their two gigantic Dalmatians, Paco and Peca, are the best.

Meeting Our Heroes

BEYONCÉ I have met every singer I have ever loved—Michael Jackson, Janet Jackson, Whitney Houston. I actually got to perform onstage with Michael, and he hugged me. I could never have imagined so many opportunities. These are the things that make me feel that dealing with the criticism, the negativity, and the rumors is all worth it. That stuff still hurts, but props from the King of Pop? It doesn't get any better than that.

JANET

MICHELLE Meeting Janet Jackson was one of my favorite moments. We were introduced to her at the TMF Awards in Amsterdam. TMF is their number one music channel—kind of like MTV. The Awards are taped live in front of fifty thousand people. It's like a great big concert. For the past few years, we've taken either one or two awards home. But even better was the advice from Miss Jackson.

She was so encouraging and positive. She told us, "You girls really need a chance to appreciate the meaning of what it is that you are doing. Take some time off and go travel the world! Don't be working all of the time, because before you know it, your youth will be gone. And you will realize that you never had a chance to reflect on what you were actually able to do with your career. If you are moving too fast and you're letting your days go right by—before you can actually sit down and get some peace and time to yourself—then you can't realize exactly what it is that you've been able to accomplish. And then it's all over with—done." I thought it was very cool of Janet to share that.

Two girls that I went to high school with dance for Janet now, and when I was home for Thanksgiving, we all went out together. They said Janet is such a down-to-earth woman—she likes to go out with her dancers and have fun. On her nights off, she says, "I am going to make sure that I have some fun tonight." I like how she became an independent woman. She's really come into her own.

WHITNEY

Beyoncé, Kelly, and I saw Whitney Houston perform "I Will Always Love You" at the BET Awards. She was onstage singing, and when she got to the part that goes "I hope life treats you kind," she pointed to us! She was singing directly to us. And indeed, life has treated us kind.

KELLY I still get excited when I talk to singers I used to listen to when I was a little kid. When I met Whitney Houston, she gave me some valuable advice. She said, "You girls just make sure you love what you are doing, and more important, make sure you have fun along the way." I have seen her several times after that, and I still zone out every time. She blows my mind, and to this day, it's still amazing to me that Whitney Houston would actually be standing anywhere near me. I never dreamed that would happen. I have memories from when I was five years old watching her sing on TV. And when I see her in my face, it freaks me out.

I will never forget one time we were walking through a hotel lobby in L.A. and there she was in the middle of the room doing an interview, and she actually stopped her interview just to talk to us. I have never heard of an artist doing that, let alone Whitney Houston. She started singing, "Say my name, say my name," but she was putting her own Whitney twist on it. I was like, "Oh my God." Then her husband, Bobby Brown, came over to us. He said, "My wife is a big fan!" I said, "Do you know who your wife is?" He laughed and said, "My wife seriously loves y'all." That may very well have been the greatest compliment of my life.

MICHAEL

And as if it couldn't get any better than that, later on, Michelle, Beyoncé, and I met Michael. That's Mr. Michael Jackson! We were all backstage at a Christmas concert in New York City. When he shook my hand, I was utterly speechless. I couldn't say a word. All I could say was "Michael!" I was like, Okay, if I die tonight, I think I will be okay. He sang to us, too: "I don't think I'm ready for this jelly." He was singing "Bootylicious"—to us! I don't think I was ready for that! And then he was like, "That's a great song." Oh, Michael knew exactly what "jelly" meant. It was clear that he understood the meaning of "Bootylicious," too. But just to clear up any possible misconceptions: jelly, for me, is my boo-tay. But jelly is different for everybody. I know for some people it's their thighs. For other people, it might be their hips. I am friends with a woman who has the cutest shape, and the cutest part of her shape is her hips—that's her jelly. And every woman, she needs to believe that it is delicious. Take some advice from me!

The Inspiration

MICHELLE My greatest musical influences were all from the church. Honestly. I would listen to gospel singers like Karen Clark-Sheard, Yolanda Adams, and Whitney Houston's mom. Another one of my favorites is Shirley Caesar—I am on her new gospel album, by the way, track number two. All those people are huge to me. I didn't really start listening to R&B until I got older.

My father used to be a DJ, so he always had crates full of albums. Not just R&B, either. He had everything from Iron Maiden to Steely Dan to America. All these groups are still in my CD collection now.

My collection starts with gospel: Mary Mary, Mahalia Jackson, Hezekiah Walker, and CeCe Winans. Some of these are autographed. Kim Burrell autographed her first album, *Try Me Again,* for me. There are lots of choirs from Chicago and New York that I love.

Then my CD collection veers into jazz and soul: Anita Baker, Sarah Vaughan, Stevie Wonder, Sade, and Dee Dee Bridgewater. Jazz has its own appeal to me. With gospel and R&B, so much of that music is often derived from the singing of other artists, but in jazz, some of the things people do with their voices are wholly original. Their voices almost become instruments. I always pay attention to the way that various chords and notes are sung. This is so weird, but if I am at a concert, most of the time I'm listening to the music instead of the singer. It is a shame, because I am a singer. But what I'll notice is a keyboard or a chord change. I listen carefully to the percussion, or the way the bass player is interacting with the lead guitarist.

In terms of actually wanting to be just like somebody, Sheila freaking E. is the bomb! The image of her that sticks out most in my mind is her playing with Prince—she was a sign of my time. She had the coolest black drum set. I saw her in one of those concert videos: Prince was cute, but I couldn't take my eyes off the percussion. Sheila E. was so good-looking, and I wanted my legs to be just like hers. My older brother could play the drums, and I would bug him all the time, "Please teach me to be a hot drummer!" But he never did. I couldn't imagine how such a beautiful lady could be on those drums. I never thought that a woman could wear lipstick and gorgeous clothes, and also play the drums like nobody's business. When she went solo, I will never forget watching her straddle and pound on a single bass drum—she was actually playing two at the same time, and her legs looked so long and perfect. If I had legs like that, I would wear short skirts, too.

I also love live music: James Brown, Aretha, the Andrews Sisters, Sam Cooke, and Donny Hathaway. Maybe that is because I grew up hearing live music all the time. In the gospel choir at my church there were people playing the organ, drums, piano, and guitar. We even had people who played trumpet or saxophone at school bring their instruments to church on Sunday morning and play along with the choir. I think it's cool when a group can incorporate a live band into one of their songs. Some of the best songs ever are Chicago's "Will You Still Love Me for the Rest of My Life?" and "You're the Inspiration." Another classic is "Hard to Say I'm Sorry." Chicago wrote so many wonderful love songs. I dig their harmonies and the lead singer's voice. It's piercing—the moment he opens his mouth, he's got me. That's the power of a great vocalist.

Anything by the producers Jimmy Jam and Terry Lewis is great. I definitely look up to them, because they have been around for a long time producing all kinds of different people. I have four CDs full of all their hit songs—well, not all of them, because with those two geniuses, the hits just keep coming.

Of course I have Patti Austin and Janet Jackson and, because I listen to all types of music, the Dave Matthews Band and Phil Collins. Even Lil' Kim. Everybody's in my CD collection. Why would I want to limit myself to just one type of music? Whenever I meet musicians and they recommend a CD for me to check out, I'll run right out and buy it. Even if it's not my thing, it's a good idea to check out what everybody else is listening to. I need to stay current.

As for contemporary artists, man, Sting is crazy. When I use the word "crazy" what I really mean is ridiculously talented. There are a few singers who have something very special about their voice, and he is one of them. It's also his image, the way he comes across—even when he is just sitting in the backseat in that Jaguar commercial. He always collaborates with other interesting artists, like on the song "Desert Rose," which was awesome. He's a hardworking legend who deserves all the respect that comes his way. That is exactly what I aspire to be.

KELLY My music will always be clean, and that goes for every rap CD in my collection. I am very aware of the music that I listen to—and who I listen to it in front of. That's an important principle of mine. I never listen to songs with curse words in them around my parents or around younger kids, because that would be disrespectful. All of my rap CDs are 100 percent clean. I have three godchildren—they're like my little clique—and sometimes I go and pick them up from school in my car. So if I'm listening to music, I make sure that there are no curse words. My nephew TJ is seven years old, and he listens to Eve and Nelly—TJ knows all their songs. But when it comes to a lyric with a curse word, he knows the clean version that edits it out. He doesn't know the dirty version, because that's not the one I have in my car. It is important to have respect for young listeners.

AMAZING GRACE

15

BEYONCÉ Destiny's Child could never have made it to where we are today without some divine inspiration and guidance. The church is such a big part of our lives that whenever possible, Kelly and I will still fly home just so we can attend service at Saint John's United Methodist Church and Michelle flies home to Rockford to go to her church. Church is where I can relieve stress, cry my eyes out, and get all the negativity out of my system. It's kind of like starting over. It's our safe place.

The pastor of the church, Rudy Rasmus, has a wonderful relationship with my father and mother. So whenever we need him to pray with us, he's always there. And I know a lot of times when we go overseas, he'll ask the whole church to pray for Destiny's Child. It's amazing to have that kind of extended family. That's a couple of thousand people. We were at the church from the very beginning, when it was only about ten people, and we've watched it grow and grow and grow.

I know some people have stereotypical notions of churches, but our church is helping the Houston community. It constructs buildings for homeless people and kids suffering from AIDS. It's unbelievable to see how many people are homeless—especially in the Houston downtown area. But it's great to see them not only getting help from the church, but to see also how they have turned their lives around after going to my church and getting to know God.

I started going to Saint John's when I was eleven. A lot of our success—actually, all of our success—is because of God. I was a part of the church choir for a couple of years. But after a while, I could never make rehearsals on Wednesdays. I didn't have the time to be in the choir full-time, because I was in Destiny's Child and either at those rehearsals or in the studio. The music at Saint John's is top notch, though.

The day I decided to get baptized is the proudest of myself I've ever been. I think that's the biggest thing I've ever done in my life, and it was hard for me to get that courage. Pastor Rasmus announced that there would be a special baptism for teenagers. I wanted to get baptized, but I was definitely too scared to go. I started crying. I was fighting myself. Something inside of me was saying, "You want to get baptized—go." And something else was saying, "No, you can't go up there. Nobody else is going. How are you going to be the first person to walk down the aisle?" Then my mom asked me what was wrong, and I didn't want to tell her, but I said, "I wanna go up there." And she said, "Well, why are you crying?" I said, "Because I don't want to go!" And she was like, "What? If something is telling you to go, then you need to go." So then I went and walked down the aisle. It was so scary for me. After I went, Kelly and the other kids went—they followed me. They must have been feeling the same thing I was feeling; until I stood up, they were too scared.

There was a little turquoise rubber pool, and one by one we repeated a scripture and then the pastor eased our heads into the water. God gave me the courage. The water caused a weird feeling, like something was being passed out of me and something new was coming in. I was born again—and that's when the drama came. Because once you get baptized, that's when Satan gets busy.

Keeping the Faith

KELLY I became a member of Saint John's about six years ago. Before that my mom wanted me to keep going to church with her, and sure, I liked her church, but I didn't feel as at home or as comfortable there. At Saint John's, I finally felt complete in the spiritual sense. The atmosphere there was so peaceful and loving, and the people were genuine. It's a wonderful environment. When I first walked into Saint John's, this feeling came over me. It's hard to describe, but I have never felt anything like that before in my life. I've witnessed so many spiritual breakthroughs that took place in that church. And personally, I noticed how much closer I got to God.

My spirituality has grown, and it continues to grow, at every service. That's what made me want to join the church in the first place. So when I finally did join, it was a pivotal moment for me. At the time, my mom was kind of hurt—parents always want you to go to the same church that they attend. Since I was not living under her roof anymore, my attending her church was especially meaningful to her. I was fourteen when I made that decision, and my mom did not exactly support it. I said, "Mom, I'm old enough to make my own decisions now, and you should be happy to know that I want to go to church, period."

"Baby, what are you doing? I want you to come to church with me," she said. And naturally I felt guilty. I wanted to make her happy, so I came up with a good idea for a compromise. I said, "We can switch off. I'll come to church with you one Sunday and then you can come to church with me the next Sunday." And we have actually ended up sticking to our promise.

Because we travel so much, we can't make it to Saint John's for church as much as we'd like. But when Beyoncé and I finally do come back, it is always positive and affirming. In other words, it's just what we need. The services cleanse us in a way. When I go there, I get so much out of the experience. I hear the cries of gratitude from the congregation and soon I am joining them, too, crying out to God and praying. That's my personal time to speak to my savior about whatever troubles might be going on in my life. Then I get to hear an incredible sermon from Pastor Rasmus, and the whole church erupts into song and beautiful children are literally dancing for joy. It is a glorious sight to behold.

Pastor Rasmus and his wife, Juanita, are such down-to-earth people (he even wears jeans and a T-shirt)—I love that and find it inspiring. They don't present themselves as holier-than-thou or untouchable to the church family. At some churches, I think the pastors feel that they cannot socialize with the congregation, which is just plain weird. But my pastor is incredibly involved in every aspect of the church. After all, he has dedicated his entire life to it. Not only has he been a guiding force in the lives of all the parishioners, a constant source of spiritual inspiration, but he has also supported so many lifesaving programs. That's yet another reason why I could not help but fall in love with the church, because it is genuinely active in the real world.

There are a lot of problems in Houston, many troubled lives, people in dire need of help, and we make an effort to reach out to them and make a difference in their lives. For one thing, Saint John's has a very progressive AIDS program. It raises awareness, and it is also a place where people suffering from AIDS can be treated. In addition to that, anyone can drop by and get tested. The church also runs shelters that feed the homeless every week. Homelessness is a problem that's not going to disappear anytime soon, but at least we are trying to do something about it. I've never seen a church like mine before. And when I did, I was instantly drawn to it. I knew I had to join it right away. Saint John's is a real blessing to Houston. I know it has helped save many lives.

SPIRITUAL AWAKENING

Pastor Rasmus and Juanita are two of the most beautiful people you could ever meet. I remember the day that I got baptized, when it was my turn and the pastor touched me to go under the water—I can't even describe the touch, but it felt as though God was working through him. It was as if I had been touched by the hand of God. And every time I see the pastor now, there is this gentle peace about him. There is so much wisdom and understanding inside that man that I can't even describe it.

The most significant spiritual breakthrough for me was when I got baptized. That was an amazing experience, because I felt like I was starting off brand-new. I remember that day so clearly. It was me, Beyoncé, and our former members LaTavia and LeToya. We all went to church together. Pastor Rasmus was talking about being baptized. He said it was our opportunity to wash all our sins away and start over again with a clean slate. He was holding a baptism specifically for teenagers, and although I was always a very good girl, I was hardly squeaky clean.

I remember that I wanted to stand up so badly, but I couldn't. I guess I just didn't have the nerve. Beyoncé did, though. She was brave enough to go first, and that's when I decided I was going to stand up, too. We were probably feeling the same emotions at the same time, but as usual, she had the courage to get up before anybody else. So LaTavia, LeToya, and I followed her lead. And as we walked down to the front of the church, I remember we were just crying and boo-hooing. I didn't know what His plans for us were, but it was obvious to me then that God was working in our lives.

Naturally, I had been baptized once before, when I was a baby. But I was so young that I don't remember anything about it. This time I knew that it was for real. It was my choice—a decision that I made for God. There was a large tub filled with water at the front of the church, where Pastor Rasmus stood. I walked down the aisle, and just setting foot in the water made my knees feel weak. Our church is the kind of church where you don't have to dress up, so we just had on our regular, casual clothes. I took a deep breath. I recall going under the water, and then coming back out and breathing and looking up at the light. It felt like new life.

The water pouring over me was the most spiritual sensation of my life. One by one, my sins were washed away. I knew God wanted to give me another chance. I knew that was His will. I felt purified as a Christian. There is nothing like that feeling of being able to start over again; even performing onstage cannot come close to that.

I know that a lot of people think that since God is a forgiving God, if you commit a sin, He tells you, you can start over. But the key is that *you* have to want to start over. You have to mean it sincerely and want it more than anything else in the world. You have to make a serious effort to seek it out, whether it's by reading the Bible more, going to church more, talking to a pastor or someone from church, or through the ritual of baptism. Some kind of spiritual awakening has to occur in your life. But first you have to be able to forgive yourself for your sins, whatever they happen to be. I think that might be where a lot of people fall short—they are not able to forgive themselves first. They just automatically want God to let them off the hook. But God says that you have to be able to forgive others as well as yourself before He can forgive you. That is the way He meant for it to be.

Saint Paul Church of God in Christ

MICHELLE I have been going to Saint Paul Church of God in Christ all my life, and now, I would go home every Sunday if I could.

At my church a lot of people get dressed up to come to service. People still wear their suits, and some real elegant ladies come in wearing hats and gloves. I dress up, too, even though the way most people there dress is more laid back these days. The young people wear T-shirts and jeans and tennis shoes. The church is okay with that. They understand that not everybody can turn up in three-piece suits. In this day and age when people are coming in off the streets wanting to be blessed, you just have to be happy that they are finding God. You know they might not have the clothes you have or the kind of cars you drive, but they still have every right to be there. That said, I don't expect a wealthy family to come to church dressed like they're homeless. The choir still wears their robes—and they can sing!

Saint Paul is a Bible-teaching church, so most of what we believe is straight from the Bible. My pastor studies and speaks from the Bible, and he doesn't make up anything. What I like most about my church is that while it teaches against certain types of behavior, it would never shun anyone. For example, they do preach against premarital sex, but if a teenager were to become pregnant and have her child out of wedlock, my church would still embrace her and her baby. Some pastors might judge people using their own personal beliefs, but not my pastor. He's a prayerful person, and he goes by what God has told him.

My pastor is very spiritual, and I know that God speaks to him. I think it's cool that he can talk about his personal experiences and how he has triumphed over the trials in his life. I think it's good that he talks about those challenges, because then other people know that they have no need to be ashamed of their own problems. Some preachers come across like they are perfect and they have never sinned, and people have a hard time relating to that. But if a pastor speaking at church can tell you how God has helped him to overcome his own struggles, you and others respond to that.

We have all kinds of people who come to my church—drug addicts who have been delivered from drugs, prostitutes who no longer walk the streets. The people at my church embrace the fact that they are not perfect. That is why they want God in their lives.

It's important to keep an open mind. If you have been cooped up in a church all of your life, you're going to think smaller than if you have gone out into the world and seen a lot of things. By going out into the world, you can get to know God for yourself. It's a shame that there are some people who spend their whole lives worrying that they are going to die and go to hell. They might think that if someone has a baby out of wedlock, that person will be headed straight to hell. Somebody might think that I am going to hell simply because of the way I dress! But I can't worry about what other people think or say about me, because in the end it's going to be just Him and me. And me and God, we're tight.

Sweet Charity

KELLY We've been so blessed that we try to give as much back to the community and fans as we can. It feels good to perform for kids from the Make-A-Wish Foundation—we always make room for them at our concerts. And we're very active in our church, of course.

Near Saint John's, we just did the groundbreaking for our youth center, which is really exciting. We're building that with some of the money we made from record sales—it's our way of giving something back to our local fans. So many kids get into trouble because they have time on their hands and no guidance in their lives. My mom was always working, so I don't know what I would have done if I hadn't met Beyoncé and her family.

The youth center is going to be a place where young kids can go instead of the street. There they can still do something fun, but it would be positive fun. The streets are filled with negativity sometimes, and this is a safe haven for them to get away from the dangerous elements like the drugs and the violence. I'm not so old that I forget what kids go through—I know that they go through a lot. If troubled young people go there because of us, and they find the encouragement they need to turn their lives around, that would be amazing. Hopefully this center will be a place where they can learn about themselves and grow spiritually, as well as have a good time.

BEYONCÉ I hope the youth center will be a place where teenagers can hang out and get their minds off any negative temptations in their lives, as well as the craziness that comes along with being that age and growing up. I don't know anyone who can look back on those years and say that it was easy. For kids who are into sports, we're building basketball courts, and I would also like to offer something that has to do with music. Ideally there will be room for a recording studio inside and that will be a big draw. So if they are more interested in what a recording studio has to offer than in sports, they deserve to have access to that, too.

My experience has taught me that if you have better things to do with your time, you can stay off the streets and away from unhealthy peer pressure. I want to set a good example, but that doesn't mean kids have to work as hard as we did in order to succeed. When Michelle was in school she treated singing as a hobby, but it was still a positive force in her life. This is our way of reaching out to kids who might not have the kind of supportive family environment that I had.

MICHELLE I'm very excited about the youth center in Houston. It's Mathew's and Tina's vision. Tina is so warm and passionate with people and especially children—that's one of her gifts. She knows how to boost their self-esteem. She makes them feel special and lets them know that they are something special. Mathew, too—there are many obstacles he has overcome. At this center, young people can come and find some type of peace and help and comfort.

Recently, when I went back home, I visited the youth outreach program in Rockford, which is called Let's Talk It Out. They meet every week and reach out to underprivileged kids in the area. I just went there on my own one day. It wasn't a big media thing—no newspaper people came out to cover it—it was basically me going there and spending time with about forty kids. We ordered food and talked. They just wanted to have a conversation with me. I also met with some kids at the Rockford Housing Authority (RHA). RHA supervises housing projects in the Rockford area. It helps kids find a place to live. They wanted me to come and speak, but when I got up in front of all of them and asked if they had any questions, they got real quiet. They were so shy! But we ended up having a lot of fun together. I think things like that can make a difference. It lets the kids know that a regular little girl like me can achieve her goals and become successful.

We all have things that we want to do in life. I just think that we have a fear of doing the initial stepping out and finding a way to do it. I want to encourage kids: Whatever it is you want to do, don't be afraid to make the first move. You might not have the money or the connections, but if you just step out on faith, you'll be where you want to be in due time.

LIFE ON THE ROAD 16

BEYONCÉ Life on the road is hard, to put it mildly. You have to be very strong to survive in this field. If you do love performing enough, it's worth it. But if you don't have a strong personality, you will be headed for trouble.

I see why so many artists get hooked on drugs and alcohol. Some performers do drugs because they need an escape from their everyday lives. Drugs are a terrible mistake. I hope I will never try any type of drug. I would be scared to be anywhere near narcotics. First of all, because they're awful. Second, I understand why a person would start to depend on them again, and again, and again, until it's too late. I can understand the feeling that makes people addicted to them—that need to get away from it all. I have felt that urge. There is so much pressure in this business, and it can seem impossible to cope with it at times. I want nothing more than to get away from that stress, and I struggle with the need to escape. There are moments when it seems like nothing can help you except running away—and some artists' way of running away is intoxication, which is ultimately self-destructive.

My form of escape is creative—I deal with my problems by writing. When things get bad, I write songs, which is why

I have written so many. That's why I wrote "Survivor." But still, you need to also have something totally outside of music. If music is your whole life, you need something besides it to comfort you.

Support Systems

In this business, you can get so brainwashed and psyched up. Imagine having everybody around you telling you how good you look all the time—"Hey, that outfit looks perfect on you!" They are essentially kissing your butt, and you start believing them. You begin to think you can't do anything wrong. Destiny's Child is lucky, because we don't have that at all. My mama's always telling me, "Beyoncé, you need to comb your hair." And my daddy's saying, "Y'all's performance was not as good as it could have been." They tell us when we perform badly, and they tell us when we do well, but they always tell us the truth.

I understand how some artists get out of touch with reality. It's because of all of the people who work for them. Some singers surround themselves with "yes" people, and all it takes is the wrong assistant to say, "You don't need to be nice to her. You're selling a lot more records than she is. And you look better, too." I have overheard many conversations like this. If that's what you hear every day, you're going to eventually start believing it. We are a product, a result, of our environment. And some artists live in unhealthy environments. Their minds get contaminated.

People on a payroll are not going to tell an artist, "You were awful tonight." They lie because they want to keep their jobs. So that's why I understand, even sympathize, with some of the singers who act like divas. It's terrible behavior, but some people are not as fortunate as we are.

FAMILY SUPPORT

MICHELLE I still need to talk to my mom and dad all the time—I'm constantly on the phone with them when I'm on tour. That's why my cell bill is so high. I'm supposed to have two thousand minutes for two hundred dollars a month, but I got a bill one day that was almost a thousand dollars. And then there is my friend the two-way pager. My two-way bill is about seventy bucks a month. Both of those are always up, twenty-four hours a day, seven days a week.

I'm constantly on the phone with my dad. It helps to talk to him. I still have a long way to go in terms of my self-esteem. I just try to remind myself that God has given me something special. He has given each of us a different gift. You just have to find it, know it, walk it, talk it, sleep it, and eat it. Don't ever forget about it and lose it. And if you live right and treat people well, then you are going to grow. No matter what it is that you want to do, your gift will make room for you in this world. I used to be the baby of the family, but now my ten-year-old sister, Danielle, is. I'm not sure that I want her to follow in my footsteps—my feet hurt from all of this running around in heels.

I'm lucky to be surrounded by encouraging people, because this job is harder than I ever could have expected it would be. My family and friends are constantly giving me support. I never think, Oh, I have got it made now. I still get lonely. I get tired, sad, and angry. And it's well known that in this industry you can get depressed—look at what happened to Mariah Carey. She had just gotten a multimillion-dollar record deal! People thought she was on top of the world.

The problem is, once people see someone on television or in concert, they forget that he or she is a human being. Some people assume that everything in my life is great because I have a video on MTV, but it is still a job. Beyoncé, Kelly, and I are normal people walking down the street, and we still see ourselves that way. I may be wearing sequins, but if you cut me, I'm still going to bleed.

I am what I am on TV and onstage, but once I get home, let me not be Michelle from Destiny's Child; just let me be Michelle, little ol' me. When I am at the grocery store buying Doritos, I just want to be myself. I am as goofy in front of the cameras as I am off, but off camera I wear a lot less makeup and more affordable outfits.

I don't like when celebrities neglect to mention their struggles. Our lives aren't all peachy and creamy. That's fake. I want to hear that you cried last night, or got out of bed in the morning and cried. Or maybe you sat in the tub and just cried—whatever. The point is you cried. Artists have feelings, and that makes us real.

THE POWER OF PRAYER

KELLY My spirituality continually inspires me. It strengthens me, and I need that strength when I'm on tour. Life on the road is hard, but I get by thanks to the amazing power of prayer. Wherever Destiny's Child goes on tour—either on a bus or on a plane—we can always rest assured knowing that our church and our pastor are praying for us. Beyoncé and I can sometimes be away from Saint John's for two months, but it always helps us to know that we are in somebody's prayers. And if I cannot make it to church, I still find wisdom and encouragement in the Bible. The scriptures provide for my needs. I try to read the Bible every day.

To be honest, because of our crazy tour schedule, I have not made it to church in a few weeks. But the past two Sundays that I have been able to attend, the sermon was exactly what I needed to hear. When we are away for long periods of time, we try to re-create the Sunday service. No matter where in the world we are, if it is a Sunday, Beyoncé, Michelle, and I will join hands and pray together just as if we were in church. It's even better if Aunt Tina or our vocal coach happens to be there. It is always good to have an adult there—in case you run into a scripture that you cannot understand, they can break it down for you.

POSITIVE DISTRACTIONS

BEYONCÉ We have so many ways of coping with the craziness of life and touring. If you have excess energy, it helps to focus it on something positive. I always try to improve my product. Even at a young age, I would think about what I wanted to achieve, and concentrate all my energy on making that goal happen. There should always be something new in life that you're trying to do. And as soon as you accomplish it, you should set another goal right away—learn how to cook, learn how to play guitar, learn how to speak Spanish—just learn how

to do something to enrich yourself. It should be something that you always wanted to do. That way when you start to feel the urge to do dumb stuff, you go and focus on your new goal. If you are busy trying to be a successful singer, you don't have free time to be doing drugs or other things that aren't going to help your career. That's what kept me on the right track.

I wasn't even distracted by boys. I was like, "Whatever. I'm trying to be a singer." So that sharp focus is what kept me away from anything bad. I'm happy that my mom suggested I take dance classes and voice lessons. It kept me busy, and it kept my mind occupied. Plus it made me want to work at it so hard that I couldn't give up. I felt like all this time I've been in voice lessons and so many competitions—I'm not about to just give up. I had better get something out of all the money I have spent. All the money my daddy spent, that is. And we have all gotten more than we ever dreamed.

Backstage Pass

KELLY Touring is a crucial part of this job. Beyoncé, Michelle, and I have always agreed that it is the best way to connect with your fans and promote your music. But it's also the toughest!

Once, when we were in Denver, Colorado, opening up for Christina Aguilera, I broke two of my toes. The lights had just gone down and I was leaving the stage to make a quick change before our encore. I was the last one off, and I couldn't see jack backstage, because it was pitch black and no one was waiting for me with a flashlight to help me find my way. I was basically following the sound of Beyoncé's and Michelle's heels clicking somewhere off in the distance. So I accidentally ran into a ramp—an *iron* ramp, the kind that is used to load all the equipment onstage. I smacked my foot right into it, and I screamed from the pain. I knew that something was seriously wrong. I had never felt pain like that before. I tried to stand up and hobble back to the stage but I just fell over, it hurt so bad. I was writhing around on the floor holding my foot, screaming, "Oh, my God, my toe is killing me!"

I looked up and there was Beyoncé standing over me, even though she had to be onstage—she was going to miss her cue. But she held my hand tight and said, "Don't worry, Kelly. I'm here. It's going to be okay. Can you wiggle your toes? Do you think they're broken?" A bunch of people ran over, they took my boot off and propped my foot on a rolled-up towel. We knew something was wrong, because my foot looked terrible. My toes were starting to swell and turn blue and purple. I sat up and I tried to put on my boot, but Beyoncé grabbed my hand and said, "Kelly, don't be crazy. You can't walk. Get your foot away from that shoe." But I just wanted to get back on that stage—the encore is my favorite part! Instead, I ended up going to the emergency room. I still had my skimpy stage costume on—who knows what the nurses must have thought. Beyoncé and Michelle had to go out by themselves for the last two songs and explain to the audience that I had just broken my toes. At least I didn't break a leg.

It took my toes three months to heal, so for the rest of the dates on that tour, I had to sing while seated on a stool. That was the worst for me, because I absolutely love doing our routines, and to be restrained from performing was so depressing. I couldn't even do the most basic dance move.

BEYONCÉ The Christina Aguilera tour was a major tour, and Kelly, Michelle, and I should have been provided with lights—even a Bic would have done the trick—but stuff like that happens. Nobody ever thought somebody would hurt their foot, but that's a very easy mistake to be made.

We were glad to at least have a dressing room. On our very first tour we didn't get so much as a broom closet to change in, because that's when we were first starting off. That was the Boyz II Men tour. We had on these white dresses with long trains, but we had to change into them outside in this little tent. Rain was pouring down and our trails were dragging in the mud—our beautiful dresses were ruined. Michelle asked me, "Oh, is this what touring is really like?" It was a letdown for all of us. But, actually, it had nothing to do with Boyz II Men. They had no idea. We ended up getting really close to them, and they helped us get a dressing room of our own. It wasn't anything fancy, but it sure beat the tent.

For our next tour, with TLC, we had a dressing room— a very little dressing room—and by the time of the Christina Aguilera tour, we had a nice dressing room. We figured you've got to crawl before you walk—you can't expect one when you first start off, and we understood that. Of course, with Kelly's accident it was almost the opposite—first she was walking and then she was crawling!

On the Christina Aguilera tour, Kelly, Michelle, and I were at a level where we should have had our own quick-change room. We have no beef with Christina, though. We considered ourselves very lucky to be on her tour—it gave us a lot of exposure.

Headliners

We love to perform for our fans, but it's not one big nonstop party like in *Almost Famous,* that's for sure—no sex and drugs and groupies for us. And if it's not your tour and you are not the headlining act, well, then you just might find out that your dressing room is a mud pit underneath a tent. That's what audiences don't realize.

Usually the headliners—and by no means am I directing this comment toward Christina Aguilera or TLC or any artist in particular, because this is true of all tours—are concerned about the possibility of being upstaged. They don't want you to look or sound better than them, so they don't allow you to have anything special. They can forbid you to have certain lights, they might not allow you to have access to quick-change booths for costume changes, they can even limit the volume of your music, and believe it or not, they can forbid you to wear certain clothes that might be flashier than theirs. If your outfits look too good, they won't let you wear them. They have all the power—complete creative control over you—because they're paying the bills.

When you're the opening act, it's hard to understand and accept that what you are allowed to do onstage is very limited. Headliners even have approval of your set—small things that wouldn't affect their performance. But if they worry that it might halfway upstage their act, then they can say, "Sorry, no way are you going to do that. You can just forget about it." That's the risk you take until you headline your own tour. And that's something we had to go through.

Destiny's Child does a lot of costume changes in between songs. That means Kelly, Michelle, and I have anywhere between thirty and forty-five seconds to get out of one outfit and into another. If we had to run all the way back to a dressing room, by the time we got there and changed, it would be too late to make it back onstage. So instead we rely on a quick-change booth—essentially a mini-tent with a couple of mirrors that's right behind the stage. There we can put on a new outfit and get back in front of the audience before they even realize we left. I think we are the fastest quick-change artists in the business, because we've been rehearsing it for many years. We're all like Wonder Woman—we just spin around and wham, we're sporting a new look!

Now that we are in the position to headline, we make sure to be considerate of our opening acts. They can wear whatever they want. Because we have such a crazy light show, we let them use our lights, which we pay thousands of dollars for every night. Some of our openers have used the lights to make a pyro effect—and for an opening act to get fireworks is unheard of. The things that we allow our opening acts to do, no other tour has allowed. But we want to help them as much as possible because we've been in their position, and it was tough. We had to endure so much creative censorship. We always said that when we got our own tour, we wouldn't be like that. Hopefully other groups will follow our lead.

What It Takes

Michelle, Kelly, and I read *Billboard* almost as religiously as the Bible. I hear about the casualties of the industry. Hundreds of artists think they've made it when they get signed to a record deal. Those contracts don't come with a lifetime guarantee, unfortunately. Normally, it's a one-album-at-a-time commitment. A year later, not many of those acts are still around. A lot of people are born with immense talent, but they don't want to work. Or they're disappointed to find out how much work it is—because it never stops.

America is enormous, and if you want to make it in this country, you have to tour everywhere. Not just New York and L.A. You need to hit all the major cities in all fifty states, and then you need to go back and do the smaller cities and towns. That's how you build buzz. Sustaining that buzz is even more work. Then you have to break the European market and Japan.

The reason Destiny's Child has such a good relationship with radio stations and our records get played so much is because when we first came out we did a free radio show in just about every big city in America. For about a year we were basically working for free. A lot of groups don't do that because, well, they want to make money. My father was smart enough to realize that if we did those shows for free, we'd build up relationships with radio stations and then they'd play our records. It worked, obviously, because all of our singles went to number one and radio stations still play them.

At the time, though, it was hard because we weren't making any money. That meant we were sharing hotel rooms, my mom was styling our clothes for free, we couldn't afford makeup artists, and my father was paying for everything out of his own pocket. He and my mom were spending hundreds of thousands of dollars! They went through their savings, and we had to move from a big house to a smaller house and sell one of our two cars. Until "Say My Name," we flew coach everywhere—Europe, Japan. We didn't have limos. We were driving ourselves around. We rehearsed in our living room, because we couldn't afford a rehearsal studio. We tried to have only one tour bus, because they cost so much. We did some little miracles in the beginning with costume changes—no designers wanted to lend us clothes. My mom had to sew our outfits by hand—that was miles of thread. Luckily, my dad and mom were really good about finding ways to save so that we could do the most with the little money we had.

Some artists don't realize that every dollar you spend comes out of your own pocket. Labels pay for videos up front, so when you start making money, you don't get it. That's why it takes so long for artists to make money. Before you can even touch the money you make, it goes to the label.

Touring is tough, because on any given day in some city, in some country, somewhere in the world, there is an important awards show or music event that you should not miss and will have to fly in for. Very often a deadline hangs over my head. There's a crucial magazine interview that I need to give. There are photo shoots, public appearances, costume fittings, and concerts. I have walked down hundreds of red carpets. Promotion allows for no downtime, and somehow I need to find time to write new songs. Sleep is an afterthought. How to sum it up: stress, stress, and more stress.

BAD PRESS

MICHELLE I'm rarely serious on TV, but every now and then I lose my patience when an interviewer disrespects my sisters. If I'm having a bad, snappy day, or I'm sad, I'm less likely to be forgiving when someone is trying to dog us. So I might misspeak on a talk show. When I have one of those outbursts, Beyoncé and Kelly will say, "You have to forgive Michelle. She didn't take her medicine today." Then afterward they'll take me aside and jokingly say, "We're going to buy a muzzle to put over your mouth. Seriously!"

One time we were doing an interview, and while Beyoncé was talking, the host of the show was looking at her like she was crazy. I tried to smile at the interviewer, but then her snarl got even uglier and more evil. So in the middle of the interview I said, "Why are you looking at Beyoncé like that?" I know I should not have let that upset me. I'm not supposed to let things like that get to me. But sometimes they do, and I have to let it out. Later, of course, I was like, Oh, my God, I can't believe I just said that on national television. But at the same time, people need to know we're real, and every now and then we might say something out of order. We may work all the time, but we're not robots or machines.

I don't keep a script in my head. And no way am I going to let anyone dog my sisters—they're family.

Blame It on Me, B-E-Y-O-N-C-E

BEYONCÉ Sometimes I feel like the media is out to get me. If I had my choice, I would rather see a bad photo of me in a magazine than read a bad story about me. I'm a singer and a songwriter, not Cindy Crawford. I wake up in the morning with swollen lips and that just-woken-up face—I do not look even remotely cute. I have been known to have an unfortunate case of bed-head, with my hair twisted in knots like an old mop. Or maybe one day I didn't have the energy to remove my foundation before I got a chance to sleep for all of three hours, so when I wake up my face is covered with blemishes. Once in a while I look downright gross. There's nothing wrong with that, because who in the world looks perfect all the time? But for somebody to make a negative remark about me—especially in print—that's my reputation, my character being called into question. And no makeup artist or hairstylist can sit me down in a chair for a few hours and then, presto, my image is as good as new again. So please, give me the bad picture any day.

VH1/ VOGUE FASHION AWARDS

Soon after the Christina Aguilera tour we had to perform at the 2000 VH1/*Vogue* Fashion Awards. We had already committed to do the show and they wanted us to perform "Independent Women Part 1" from *Charlie's*

Angels. Since Kelly had a broken toe, we had to completely change the routine. We didn't know how we were going to pull it off. Finally we came up with the idea to reenact the video, singing while we were sitting at a conference table, which was the only practical solution, since Kelly couldn't stand up, let alone dance. I thought it was clever. Somehow we got through that performance and all the models and fashionistas in the audience loved it. But the next day, instead of hearing people telling us how well we did, all we heard were rumors that I was the one who had broken Kelly's toe. There were so many rumors flying around after the VH1 performance. One said that I was jealous that Kelly danced better than I did; another said that Kelly broke her toe on purpose just to get attention and sympathy. Man, that was the nuttiest thing I've ever heard of in my life.

IN THE STUDIO

People have this image of me as a blond dictator in the studio. They think I tell Kelly and Michelle, "I don't care what it is you have to say—I'm going to write this entire album myself." But that's not how it works.

Writing is a weird thing. With some artists, somebody will write the chorus for them—that's the hard part and the most important, because it repeats. A few artists don't write their songs, but they will write two words or maybe a sentence. For instance, instead of saying "outside" they may ask, Can we say "inside"? If they do that, they still get writer's credit even though it might only be half of one percent of the creative contribution. When the CD lists the writers' credit for a song, that person's name is there.

A few people like to say, "Beyoncé didn't write her own songs." But there isn't anybody else in the studio but Kelly, Michelle, and me. Here's how it works: First of all, the music tracks come in and each of us has access to them. Everybody has the opportunity to contribute lyrics. I'm the first to get at it—I might be on a plane or in a makeup chair, or even in the bathroom, wherever. An idea for a song pops into my head, and I write it down on whatever I have available, whether it's a notebook or a napkin. Then I'll keep fleshing out the idea, hammering out the lyrics, until I have an entire song. (I produce some of the music, too.) Then I'll tell the girls, "I wrote a little something. Y'all want to hear it? Will you sing it?" Kelly and Michelle will say, "Oh, absolutely. Let's do it!" It's not any kind of competition. We never argue or fight for control, and that's something that I want everybody to know.

The ability to put a song together is a gift, just like being able to cook—it's as simple as that. Writing songs is something that I was meant to do. Some people can write their own material, and some people cannot. Just like some people can write a book, and some people can't. If I tried to write a novel it would probably be terrible, because I write what I know—besides, what Destiny's Child has been through is stranger than any fiction.

Even being the lead singer of this group is not something I chose. It's not something that my daddy demanded. He never insisted, "My daughter will always sing lead." Before my father even started managing us, I sang the lead. And when we enter the studio with producers, my father is seldom there. The producers choose who sings the lead part. That's not something that I would fight over, because it's just more work. When I first started out in Girl's Tyme, we would all be in the studio together and Alonzo Jackson, the producer, would say, "Beyoncé, you should sing this song." I never, ever wanted to upstage anyone. That's why for a long time, I held back. I didn't sing as powerfully as I could, because I didn't want to stand out. It's just really disappointing and hurtful that people have this warped vision of what the studio process is like.

If anyone watched the TV show *Pop Stars,* that series revealed how it really is. None of those girls walked into the studio and decided, "I'm going to sing the lead." The producer said to each one of the girls, "Go in there and sing the song." And whoever sang it the best—and the way that the producer wanted it to sound—was the person who got the lead part. It didn't have anything at all to do with the girls. So that's how it works. That's a perfect example. I hope people are finally realizing the truth.

Now that I am producing our own records, I ask the other girls to sing all the time. I don't want to sing all the leads myself. It's exhausting. Their voices deserve to be heard—they're beautiful, and I think it adds so much to the group.

On *Survivor,* Kelly sang lead on eight of the songs, but nobody ever mentioned that. (Kelly sang a lot on the last two records, and even on the second one, she sang lead on "Bills, Bills, Bills.") Kelly sings lead on "Bootylicious" and "Independent Women." For "Bootylicious," she sings the first and second verses, and I sing one of the B sections and Michelle sings the other B section. The same thing for our song "Survivor." We sing equally throughout the CD. On the Christmas record we all had songs where we each sang lead by ourselves. Critics just don't always acknowledge that, and it really makes me mad.

A few reviewers made it seem like I was a microphone hog. It was like they didn't want to even give credit to Kelly, and she sounded wonderful. They wrote things like, "Beyoncé, why don't you ever share the vocals?" As if Kelly wasn't there. And that really made me mad. This even happened after "Emotions" came out, and we each sing the same amount on that song: Kelly sings the first verse, I sing the second verse, and Michelle sings the second bridge. There was a rumor that the reason why Michelle was singing lead on some songs is because she was messing with my mama. On the Internet there were things like, "It's because Beyoncé's mama told Beyoncé she had better let Michelle sing lead—'cause that's her woman." It's insane and wildly untrue! What they should have said but didn't was that Michelle was singing lead because she is talented and deserves the opportunity.

Still, when the CD was released some people were like, "Beyoncé is showing off again." Even though it's not like that. I've never thought I was better than anybody else. And I have to live my life trying to prove that to people. I can't win. Critics want to make me out to be a diva control freak, and that misconception has gotten in people's heads. It's very irritating.

In the past, I have turned down opportunities to do solo projects. When we were first trying to get a deal, some labels just wanted me, and I didn't go for that. I didn't want to be alone. I wanted to be in a group. So for people to say I have used Destiny's Child to launch my solo career is just ridiculous, because I never had to be in this group. I chose to be in it. I love this group, and I needed my girls to be my friends and my partners. I love Kelly and Michelle, and I enjoy singing with them. I don't understand how I could be using them. We all sing. I write and produce the songs. It's ridiculous and disappointing to keep reading those lies. Some people in the media must do it because they are hoping the group will get mad at me, or I will get mad at them, and eventually it will separate us. But it won't; we're too tight.

IN THE MEDIA

I had a similar problem when we performed on TV. There was so much pressure on me. People would always say things like, "Why do they only show you on camera?" That wasn't my choice. I wasn't directing the show. I didn't tell them to just show me. My daddy didn't say, "Give Beyoncé a close-up—forget about the rest." The cameramen get their direction from the show's producer. And that's terrible, because Kelly and Michelle spend the same amount of time in the hair and makeup chair and they have just as much to say as I do. So if the show airs and it's just my face on screen, then all their preparation was for nothing.

Now, a few TV shows actually do their research and know enough to cut to the other girls, but most of the time, that's not how it turns out. It's not my fault, so I wish people would stop blaming me. If anything, there have been numerous occasions where I have walked up to producers myself, shook their hand and said, "Look, the last time we did this show, y'all showed Kelly and Michelle, but not as much as you should have, so please, please give the other girls equal time. This is not the Supremes."

We always show one another support, and because of that, one magazine said that Kelly and Michelle are "nauseatingly appreciative" of me—in other words, we get along. We don't hate one another and have catfights. We just show one another love. Another magazine wrote, "Destiny's Child are so overly supportive, it's enough to make you sick." I guess they found it disappointing that we don't argue. Not only that, but we will go out of our way to help one another out. When Kelly wanted to do a solo song, she asked me to write it. I know her well enough that I could, and I went to watch her recording sessions. When Kelly did the video, I went to the shoot to keep her company. When I did *Carmen*, Kelly and Michelle both came to visit me on the set. The press doesn't want to report stuff like that. They only want drama, because drama sells magazines and newspapers. I understand that, but journalists have got to take some responsibility. They need to understand that they are messing with people's reputations—people's lives—by painting these pictures that do not reflect reality. They are so quick to print negative rumors, but positive things, never. You don't hear about all the charity events we do. They would much rather dwell on the member changes and the drama that we went through years ago, even though it's over and means nothing to us anymore.

There's no more drama, but the media still likes to report little things to mess with our minds, like "Here is a photo of Beyoncé and her elves." That shows such disrespect to my sisters—referring to two incredible singers as "elves." So many groups don't survive in this business because they let comments like that get to them. But we understand the games that the media plays. It still hurts, especially when our families and friends see it. They don't always understand. Some people believe everything they read. Those are the ones who read a gossip item in a tabloid, then get in your ear and tell you, "Why did that magazine call you one of Beyoncé's elves?" They don't understand that whoever wrote the article is just hoping to sell magazines. I'm not responsible for that comment. It's clearly not a quote from me. I would never say something like that. But we don't let it affect us. We're much smarter than that.

CENTER STAGE

Another misconception about me is that I try to draw attention to myself and away from the other ladies. How untrue! I don't go out of my way to stand out, even with my clothes. People have tried to say, "Beyoncé always gets to wear the best outfits." But we all wear the same clothes. We never argue about who gets to wear what. I might wear a dress, Kelly will wear hot pants, and Michelle will put on regular pants—that's not because she's not hot, it's because

that's what she's comfortable wearing. It's all made from the same material. For the Grammys, we each had on look-alike outfits but with different shoes. Sometimes it feels like no matter what, I can't win. If I don't look good, then haters say, "Beyoncé looks ugly." And if I do look good, then they say, "Beyoncé's trying to outdo the other girls." What am I supposed to do? My costumes have never been any more special or spectacular. For the "Say My Name" video, we all wore Roberto Cavalli pants with matching tops. In "Jumpin' Jumpin'," I had on a Christian Dior bathing suit top and a Christian Dior belt, but my skirt was not high-end—it came from my closet and it cost about twenty dollars. Kelly wore a Christian Dior neckpiece that was worth twenty thousand dollars—that was more than my whole outfit put together. And, hello, that was just a necklace! But nobody noticed that.

We were recently on *TRL* and Carson Daly asked, "Who's the biggest flirt?" Everybody in the audience yelled out, "Beyoncé!" He asked, "Who's got the worst habits?" Everybody yelled, "Beyoncé!" Carson said, "Who eats the most?" Everybody yelled out, "Beyoncé!" I was like, Oh, my God. What do I not do wrong? Come on now! Fingers always get pointed in my direction. That's why I wrote the lyrics for the song "Dot." "If something's wrong, blame it on me: B-E-Y-O-N-C-É." Thankfully, Kelly and Michelle understand. The key to our success is that we communicate with one another. We really need one another, and that's why we are so close. We trust, believe in, and support one another. That's the only way this can work.

Never Give Up

I have wanted to give up so many times. I mean, still, to this day, there are times when I feel like I want to call it quits. Those are the days that I'll pick up a magazine and read some awful quote that I never said, or see that someone, perhaps a peer, dissed me, or else a writer just makes up an ugly lie, like when *Rolling Stone* printed a story about how I was drinking champagne at one of Wyclef Jean's parties. Everyone knows I don't drink alcohol. My drink of choice is a Shirley Temple. Or maybe I'll see some singer I was looking forward to meeting. I'll smile at her and say hi, and she'll give me nothing but attitude and shady looks—maybe she won't even bother to take off her sunglasses and make eye contact. All that stuff, it comes in clumps, and it gets me down.

That's when I go back to my room and lie down on my bed and think, you know what, this job is just not worth it. But I know that's bull, because it really is worth it to me. And it's worth it to the fans. Some days, I don't want to get out of bed, especially the early mornings when I have nothing to look forward to but sixteen hours on an airplane. The wake-up call rings at 4:00 A.M. and I want to throw a pillow at the phone, because the fatigue wears me down and makes me cranky. Every now and then, I don't even have time to take a shower before I have to leave for the airport. But then right when I'm feeling like I can't go on, I'll meet somebody from the Make-A-Wish Foundation or a similar organization who reminds me why it's all worth it. I'll call up a young girl in a wheelchair who is seriously ill, and she's so happy because she wanted to get a phone call from Destiny's Child. Or maybe I'll meet a man at an autograph signing who will start crying and tell me he is a recovering alcoholic and that he listens to "Survivor" every morning. He'll say that song helps him get through the day without drinking, and he's been sober for three months now. To have that effect on somebody's life, to be able to ease their pain just a little bit by talking to them, that is what really matters. It makes me stop and think that I am not going to let whatever little problems I have stop me. It makes me feel better, as good as the first time I ever stepped onstage.

I have my bad days. I have my insecurities. It's really easy for me to listen to that voice that tells me I can't do something. That voice can consume me with doubt. It says, "Naw, you can't do it, Beyoncé. They don't like you." Then I might read something negative about me or the group, or I may speak to somebody who is bitter. And I let it get me upset, it gets blown out of proportion, and it eats away at my confidence. But then I'll go and perform in front of twenty thousand screaming people who are holding up hand-painted "I love you, Destiny's Child!" signs. That's when I realize that so many more people love me than those unhappy people who hate me. The people who don't like me do so for no good reason at all. Some of them have never met me, and even if they did and we got along fine, they still wouldn't like me. Because then they would have to admit that they were wrong. They like the distorted picture of me they have in their minds, that's the image they would rather see.

Star Treatment—Not Really

People think that just because we're well known, Kelly, Michelle, and I get fabulous free clothes sent to us all the time. Donatella Versace may work with my mother to design gowns for the Grammys, but some of our outfits come from the sale rack at Contempo Casuals. Although we used to love shopping—and sometimes we still do run out "quickly"—my mom usually hits the malls alone. Shopping isn't a carefree and fun experience for us anymore.

Not too long ago, we did make it out on our own to Patricia Field's store in Greenwich Village, and everybody was super-duper nice to us. We were looking for wild outfits and wigs to wear in the "Bootylicious" video. The director, Matthew Rolston, thought it would be funny if I sported a Mohawk. I wasn't sure if I could work that look, so I went to check out the Mohawk wigs. After we were finished running up our credit card bills downstairs, we went upstairs, where they have a mini hair salon. We just fell in love with that store. I asked the drag queen behind the counter if I could please try on the Mohawk wig. And Miss Thing had herself a little attitude problem. She looked down at her fake nails and pretended not to hear me. I was just like, Golly, sorry to bother you.

Eventually she helped me out and allowed me to try the wig on. I thanked her and asked her for her business card, because I wanted to go back and get a black wig for a disguise. A few months later a story came out in *Spin* magazine that reported our shopping spree. It said that Destiny's Child "were ghetto bitches with no class! Beyoncé's mom does her extensions, and you can totally tell." They actually called us "ghetto bitches!" And I was like, Oh, my god, what is this? The salespeople were so nice to us, and we had fun in there and were cool with everybody. It was our favorite new store, and we had dropped a ton of money in there. We even wore the clothes in our video. It was just unbelievable, so I didn't know where that story came from.

And then I remembered the salesclerk upstairs was kind of mean. That's when I looked at the name quoted in the story, and it matched the name on the card. My mom called up the store, and the "woman" claimed it must have been a misquote—but whatever. The magazine still printed it, and then the *New York Post*'s Page Six picked it up as if it was a true story. Patricia Field told my mom she was very sorry, and she sent us a letter of apology. Unfortunately, *Spin* never printed a retraction in the magazine, so all of their readers believed it. It was really tacky that they put in the word *ghetto,* but the whole thing was a vicious lie that should have never appeared in print.

Not So Friendly Skies

KELLY It's not just stores that mistreat us, either. To this day, we have problems with some airlines whenever we call to request special services. "Special services" is something that all music groups request—it's just a request for an airline representative to escort you through the lines and security checks. They still go through our bags and everything, but they make sure that we don't get stuck in a long line and miss our flight. It's no disrespect to the people who have to wait in those lines. We're just always in a hurry, and if we ever missed our flight, we could possibly disappoint thousands of fans by missing out on a performance.

Once, a representative from one of the airlines told us that they don't provide special services for R&B groups. We weren't asking for tea service and gold carts to roll us around! We are not the type of people who want to be waited on hand and foot—we can do things for ourselves. We were simply asking someone to help us get through the gates on time. That one day was so swamped with appearances that we were really rushing, and in a case like that we can't just cut through the lines and ask people to move. We need someone official from the airlines to escort us through the security checks quickly and easily. But since the airline representative wouldn't help us out, we had to risk being made even later, because we had to ask our management to call up for us and say that we were pop artists. When we presented ourselves as a pop group that needed special services, they said, "Of course, no problem. We'd love to help you." The fact that such blatant racism exists in 2002 is unbelievable. No matter how many awards we win and records we sell, we still have to put up with it. So much for first class.

A DATE WITH DESTINY

18

MICHELLE In the music industry, guys are much shyer than anyone would expect. We hardly ever get approached. Maybe I should look in the mirror before I go out just to make sure I don't have any boogers sticking out of my nose, because I don't get approached at all. Sometimes I wish guys would come up to me. We're all old-fashioned that way. We'd be afraid to make the first move, but I think that's what we would have to do, since guys are too scared to come up to us. The most I have ever done was, in passing, give an extra wave of the hand that said: "Hi, I think you're cute. Come talk to me." It didn't work.

KELLY On rare occasions, when a boy does approach us, we have to be careful and guarded. Usually I can get a vibe off a guy, and I know exactly where he is coming from and whether or not he's my type. I don't really have time to date much, but if I did, I wouldn't let him in my business, no matter what. I think that if a guy likes me, then he's going to like me for who I am, not because of my career. It should just be about him and me. He doesn't have to get involved in my work in order to learn more about me. A man never lets a woman influence any of his decision making, unless maybe they're married, and even then sometimes men won't listen to what their wives have to say. But if a woman lets a man get in her ear, sometimes she gets silly and forgets her own goals. She'll listen to everything he says and let him corrupt her. Fortunately, we've been taught better than that. We love our careers and we're not going to let any guy jack that up.

Love Me, Love My Friends

BEYONCÉ Sometimes this job makes it hard for me to trust people. When I meet guys and try to feel them out, they're like, "God, Beyoncé, you act just like a guy!" When I ask them what they mean, they'll say, "You're like a guy, because you don't believe anything I say!" And I do have to be guarded for a certain amount of time before I can trust somebody. It seems impossible to find a man who is sincere and really likes me for me and not for my career. I never know anybody's ulterior motives.

I have met a few actors out in Hollywood, and the thing about the really talented ones is that you can never be certain when they're acting and when they're for real. That's kind of scary. It's also tough to tell with men in the music industry. A guy may act like he really wants to talk with me, but then it turns out it was just because he was hoping somebody would see us and take our picture together and it might help boost his career.

Guys can also be controlling. A lot of times guys like to tell you how your job needs to be done, and how they can help you improve it. They want to give you advice on everything, from how you should wear your hair, to what kinds of songs you should sing, to who your friends should be. That's how a lot of guys are. I'm not saying that you can't fall in love and then take some suggestions if they really are good ideas. But you have to be able to realize the difference between somebody who loves and cares about you and offers you a helpful suggestion, and some guy who just wants to run your life.

My rule is, if a guy says one comment about Kelly or Michelle that's not positive, it's over! It's not that he's got to sing their praises all the time and say things like, "Oh, I love Kelly and Michelle!" Nothing like that, but any negative remark about my girls results in instant dismissal, because our relationship should not have anything to do with Destiny's Child. I don't like to mix my personal and professional lives.

Looking for Mr. Right

MICHELLE The older I get and continue to work in the industry, the more I want to be loved and have someone in my life to share things with. And I want to know that it's for real. Because I do get lonely sometimes—this can be a lonely business. That's why I'm so happy for Britney Spears and Justin Timberlake. It's so cute how they support each other's careers and make time for each other in their lives. If Britney is in the recording studio, Justin will drop by for like five minutes and surprise her. It's those little minutes that can mean so much. That's why I could never say that I would refuse to have a relationship with anybody in the industry. Although it would be hard—there may be times when you're at home, but they're not, and then when they're home, you're not—but you would still have a mutual understanding of the work that goes into having a successful career.

For one thing, you would understand why that person's schedule is so busy. Right now, while we're still young, we've got to work hard, because we know that relationships come and go. Our careers are the priority, so we have got to be careful not to let relationships blindside us and take the focus off our work. We're not going to be doing this forever—our schedules won't be this busy when we're older. And then, I guess, that's when the more serious relationships should come, because then we'll be able to offer our undivided attention.

My parents' marriage has been a huge inspiration to me. They have been married for twenty-seven years. They weren't high school sweethearts, but they did meet on the school bus. At that time, my mom wouldn't give him the time of day, because she was a senior and he was an underclassman. They both went to Rock Valley Community College, where they started dating. They got married soon after she graduated from college. They have had their share of struggles, but somehow they managed to work through them. As a matter of fact, most of the marriages in my family have worked out.

I'm realistic when it comes to marriage. I know it's not all fun for my parents. They still disagree on issues and have arguments, but at the end of the day, they have put so much into that marriage that they won't turn their backs on it. Even if my dad got angry with my mom, one of the things on his mind would still be: "I really love my wife, and I'm not going to let a silly remark destroy our marriage." They love each other, so they work out what's bothering them. After all, they've got children to think about, too. I'm sure there were times when one of my parents wanted to be like, "Look, I'm leaving. I'm out of here." But they didn't. They stuck it out, and they made sure to be there for their kids, too. The point is, no one is perfect. People make mistakes, and in a relationship you have to figure out how to work it out.

CARMEN CHAMELEON

19

BEYONCÉ I am surprised that MTV approached me, let alone thought of me, to play the title character in *Carmen: The Hip-Hopera*. Carmen is not a role model by any means, whereas I have always tried to be one. She is a devious and shady lady. As flattered as I was by the offer, I wasn't sure if I should accept it. I was hesitant, because that part was basically the opposite of my image. By taking the role, I hoped that I might be able to tone down some of the real nasty traits. I had to schedule several meetings with the director about the vision he had for Carmen, and he actually let me calm her down a lot. I added a little softness to her—even with the way she treats guys, which was meant to be harsh. Originally in the script, Carmen was pure evil. She had no redeeming qualities. She had absolutely no sympathy or love for anybody, herself included. I have known a few women like that, but it's not that interesting to play such a one-dimensional role. I wanted some sweetness filtered into the character. Even though her actions were wrong, she still had a sensitive side. I tried to make her more human and less cold.

The other part of the script that worried me was the seduction scene. That was a compromise, too. The director wanted it to be more explicit than I did, but I still had to make it look realistic. I knew that in order for me to seduce a guy, I would have to do something that was, well, seductive. At the same time I had to maintain my image and not do anything that I wouldn't want kids to see. I was not about to participate in an R-rated love scene, and yet, if I wanted to be an actress, a real actress, I had to play this part. I had to realize that I wasn't playing Beyoncé; I was playing Carmen. She is not a Disney character! This movie was a lot sexier than *Snow White*.

I learned more in the three-month period of time that I was filming *Carmen* than I have learned in the past year. I had never been in a setting that different, and I was very aware of how I reacted to such a foreign environment. I felt like a fish out of water. I had to find my footing on unfamiliar terrain. I wasn't comfortable, but I was surprised by how quickly I was able to adapt.

On My Own

For the first time in my life, I was by myself when I was on the set of *Carmen*. Kelly wasn't sleeping in the bed across from mine. My sister, Solange, wasn't down the hall in her room blasting her rock music—I really missed that. My mom wasn't downstairs in the kitchen cooking me dinner. My dad wasn't in the living room watching TV. I couldn't run to him for a hug and a pep talk. If I felt lonely and I wanted company, there were only three people around: me, myself, and I. It was very tough.

I hadn't been away from Kelly in at least a decade. I have spent just about every day of my life with her since I was nine. She might have gone out of town for a week or something like that, but the longest we were ever apart was maybe two weeks tops. Suddenly there I was, alone and away from my mom and dad, Solange, Kelly, and Michelle for twelve weeks. After about a month, they came

to visit me on the set, and I have never been so glad to see them.

I appreciated the chance it gave me to learn more about myself. It taught me to grow up a little. I learned to be more responsible—everything from getting myself to the set on time (Mom wasn't around to shake me awake in the morning and cook me scrambled eggs for breakfast) to making adult decisions. I had to talk to directors, learn how to communicate my concerns, and speak up for myself. Essentially, I grew up a lot, as both a woman and as a businesswoman. I had to discuss every little detail of the part with the producers and the MTV people. I had to make smart business decisions. I have always made them in the past, but this time my dad wasn't around to advise me. I could have called him on his cell—he's always just a phone call away—but I resisted the temptation. Suddenly I was making up my own mind and learning to trust my judgment.

Even just going to interviews by myself was scary. People wouldn't expect that from me, but I was terrified when it came time to do the first interview by myself. It was the first interview I ever had to do that had nothing to do with Destiny's Child. I kept wondering why the interview felt so weird: Why couldn't I answer the questions right away? I kept hesitating and stumbling on words. Then I realized it was because my security blanket wasn't there—my girls, Kelly and Michelle, weren't around to cover for me if I needed it. I felt vulnerable. I was stuttering. The interview seemed to last forever. And at the time, I didn't even realize why. I mean, I had done interviews by myself before, all three of us have. But the subject of those interviews had always been Destiny's Child. Now, no one was asking about the group, so it was different and awkward. I had to field all these personal questions that I had never been asked before, and sometimes there was no way of getting around them. After each interview I thought, What is wrong with me? Why did I just suck so badly? And I realized that it was because I was no longer in my comfort zone. And so naturally I felt really uncomfortable.

Making Friends

I missed my girls while I was on the set of *Carmen*. I may have been lonely at first, but I tried to look at that as a challenge. It was refreshing to have to go out of my way to get to know other people and become more social. I am not a loner, but at the same time I am not what you would call a social butterfly. I haven't had the time to be exposed to a lot of people outside of my family and my group. Ever since a very young age, I've been so into my music and pre-occupied with writing and singing that, I never had free time to just kick back and hang out with people I didn't know.

Whenever I shake somebody's hand, in the back of my mind I'm thinking that they have no idea who I am. Most people think they know who I am because of what they have read and seen on TV, and they base their decision as to whether or not to like me on that. So I feel like I have to watch every little thing I do because it will most certainly be criticized. My downtime during *Carmen* forced me to learn how to talk to people, let my guard down, and be myself—all of that stuff that most girls probably learn how to do when they're thirteen.

I made a lot of new friends on the set. I had to work with different makeup artists, wardrobe stylists, a director, a producer, and an entire cast. We became very close and we still keep in touch. It's encouraging to know that there are good people out there who are genuinely nice and don't have ulterior motives. You do have to be very careful, but there *are* decent people in the industry.

THE DAYS THE MUSIC DIED

20

MICHELLE I admired Aaliyah so much, and I would have loved to have had the opportunity to sit down and talk with her and get to know her. She wasn't that much older than me, but I still consider her one of my role models. Before I joined the group, when Aaliyah first came out, I loved her and I wanted to be like her. She could do so many things—singing, dancing, and she was also a great actress. Her death really upset me. I felt like the world lost someone who was on her way to becoming a mega-superstar. Some people have said that I look like her, and that's a great compliment, because she was beautiful. We lost a true angel in that tragic plane crash, and her accident did affect how I feel about flying. But I can't let fear stop me.

When we travel, we are comforted by knowing that we have people back home who are praying for us and for all of the other people in the world who are traveling. And we pray too, but God has the last say. He already knows how you're going to die, and when you're going to go. If it is my time, well, then I'm going. There's nothing that I or anybody else can do to keep someone from dying if it's time. You can keep people on a respirator only for so long; it may be keeping them alive, but that's not the same as them being able to live and breathe on their own. They're just living off electricity. But you also can't live in fear of dying. I want to live for a long time, but if my time comes earlier than expected, then oh, well. All I can do is pray that God will protect all life and that nothing bad will happen.

KELLY Man, I remember we were on the tour bus when we found out the news. A friend of mine paged me and said: "Please tell me the Aaliyah rumor is a lie." And I wrote back: "What are you talking about?" We all got emotional right then, because it was so scary to even hear about it. We turned on the TV and saw it on the news. Sadness swept over our bus. Everybody was crying. At that point in time we realized how truly blessed we are and how your life can be taken away so fast that you have to try to live every day at your best.

I love the fact that Aaliyah's spirit was so beautiful, and she embraced everybody she met. She made you feel special when you met her. She's definitely an angel. I know that she's in heaven now, because she always brought smiles to people's faces. My most memorable time with her was when Destiny's Child first broke out and "No, No, No" became a hit. We were doing a video and working with Aaliyah's choreographer, Fatima Robinson, on the dance moves. Who was there with us in the rehearsal room rewinding the tape for us? Aaliyah! First of all, I was like, How is it that Aaliyah is sitting up there rewinding our tape? You know, she didn't have to do that. It just goes to show how humble she was. She was cool and asked us, "Hey, do y'all wanna hang out?" It was in L.A., and I remember everything like it was yesterday. She picked us up at the Bel Age Hotel. She had just gotten her driver's license and was all excited to drive. She was so sweet. We went to Roscoe's Chicken & Waffles to eat— she loved sweet food, breakfast food. She kept saying, "I love waffles, I love waffles!" And she loaded her plate. We sat down and talked, and I felt like I could just spill my guts out to her. She was just a lot of fun and I couldn't help but love being around her. She just had this light, and she always let it shine, really.

BEYONCÉ The first time we met Aaliyah was at an awards show, and she was so nice to us— truly nice. We got her number. Then when we came to L.A., and her choreographer, Fatima, was doing our routine, Aaliyah came to our rehearsal. We were rehearsing for the video shoot for "Get on the Bus," from the *Why Do Fools Fall in Love* soundtrack. We were newcomers, and she was a big star. She had hits on the radio, but she was sitting on the floor rewinding the tape for us. It was so sweet of her to do. She even drove us around the city. We all went to the Beverly Center, and she bought a parrot because she wanted to give it to one of her friends as a gift, and then we went to a video shoot for a song Timbaland was producing. Every time I saw Aaliyah, she was happy and had this presence that few people have. I feel really blessed that I met her. She was definitely an angel, and I know that God doesn't let too many of His angels go. He let her stay with us for a little while, but He wanted her back.

Her tragedy hit close to home, because we shared the same lifestyle. We had the same makeup artist, Christopher Maldonado, who also passed in the crash. Christopher did our makeup for our first video. We had just worked with him again a couple months before the accident. I have trouble sleeping on planes now. I try to watch the movie if there is one. I get bored and anxious to get off the plane. There was not only Aaliyah's accident, but then 9/11 right after that. She passed a few weeks before my birthday. I remember that my mom threw me a surprise twentieth birthday party in New York after the 2001 MTV Video Music Awards, and she almost didn't have it because everybody still felt so bad. The whole awards show had a weird vibe. Aaliyah was just such a special person, and she had a positive impact on a lot of people.

September 11, 2001

KELLY One date that I will never ever be able to forget is September 11. The worst part about it for us was that the family was not together: When we found out about the attacks, Beyoncé, Michelle, and I were in L.A., Tina was in Houston, Solange was in Seattle, and Mathew was all by himself in New York, and we were all so scared for him. Lance Bass from 'N Sync—he and I are really cool, he's my boy (but not my boyfriend despite what the tabloids claim)—two-wayed me a message that said: "Look at the news!" And I didn't read his message at first. But it kept on going off. Lance kept paging me and asking, "Where are you? I want to know where you are right now." And I paged him back and he kept telling me to turn on the news. So I turned on the TV and that was right when the second plane was hitting the tower. It affected me so much, and I feel like it's still affecting me to this day. It's just crazy. It made me feel so afraid. So many people died on those planes and in those buildings, and people were saying that L.A. would be the next target.

I spent that morning sitting in my hotel bedroom and praying. I was stressing out and crying. And then I called Beyoncé and Michelle and told them to call everybody they care about and tell them that they loved them. If you have not forgiven somebody, you need to get over it and do that right now, because you never know if your life is going to be cut off in just a minute, tomorrow, two days, or twenty years. So I called everyone I could to tell them I loved them. First, I called my mom, and she said, "Baby, where are you?" And I said, "Mom, I'm okay. I'm in L.A."

Since the airports were shut down, we drove to Houston two days later. All of our performances and promotional work that had been planned got canceled. We had a major European tour scheduled for fall, and it really hurt to have to cancel it. We hardly ever cancel an appearance, and we were excited to be going overseas. We have so many international fans that we felt that we had to go thank them and see their countries. So we postponed our tour until spring 2002, and set to work finding ways to help all those who were affected by the attack.

Now, I'm not so much scared of planes, but the anthrax scare really affected me, because, naturally, I am a very touchy person. I like to hug people. There's nothing like giving a fan a warm hug—then they walk away feeling that meeting us was genuine. We want people to be happy when they meet us. But we had to be really careful following the anthrax mailings. We couldn't even sign as many autographs for people who came up to us on the street. Everyone was telling us: "You cannot do this, you cannot do that. What if they have anthrax on them when you shake their hands?" It's crazy to have to worry about that. The whole world had just gotten crazy. But the music helps to keep me sane. And I hope that our music has the same effect on our fans.

MICHELLE I flew just two days after the attacks. I had to have faith in God. I wanted to go home to Rockford and I told myself, "I am going to make it home." That way, if something else happened after I got there, at least I would be with my family when it happened. I don't doubt my faith in God. My faith has brought me this far, so I can't doubt it now, when something tragic happens in the world. That's when the real test of your faith comes, when something like the terrorist attacks happen. When everything is going well, some people kind of forget about religion and they take God for granted. But the moment something goes wrong, that's when people realize that they need to trust in God. Ultimately, He has control over everything.

BEYONCÉ September 11 was a dramatic, terrible, unbelievable day. Watching TV was like a bad movie and my dad was in New York at the time! He would try to call me every hour. He was scared, but he didn't let it show—my mom was the one who told me. He was in the Sony building, and everyone there had to be moved down to the basement.

I found out about the World Trade Center when Angie, my cousin and assistant, called my room and told me to turn on the TV. We were in L.A. for the Latin Grammy Awards, and we were terrified. The Latin Grammys immediately got canceled. Yvette, our publicist, was with us. She was crying because her family lives in the New York area. I was worried about my family. My mom was in Houston, and my sister was somewhere in Seattle. The four of us have never before been in different cities on the same day. All I could think about was how I just wanted to go home. We prayed with my mom on the speakerphone so many times, and I kept calling my dad and my sister to make sure they were okay. As soon as we could, we loaded up the tour bus and drove back to Houston. It was so wonderful to be there with my family.

We had to get on a plane not long after that, so that we could perform at 9/11 benefit concerts in New York and Washington, D.C. In D.C. we sang "Survivor," which we weren't going to do, because we hadn't performed it in forever. We didn't have our backup dancers and we were used to doing it as the tour version. But my dad said, "You know how many people out there feel like survivors and need to hear that song?" This was in the elevator in our hotel, as we were heading down to our car. And we were like, "Okay, you're right." And we did it. It was the best crowd response and energy ever for that song because it was so real and so many people felt it. I couldn't be afraid to get on a plane—no one really knows when their time is near. Some people say that if they knew it was their last day, they would run out and do something crazy, and others would try to live that day right, so they could go to heaven. I want to make sure that I'm living it right all the time. So that if something happens, I know where I'm going.

THE BENEFIT CONCERTS

KELLY What was most memorable about the benefit concert in NYC is the fact that there were so many firemen holding up these incredibly sad signs—and in the middle of performing a song like "Emotions," that's a hard thing to see. It really made us feel the song. I mean, we always felt the song, but this time we felt it in a different way. We felt how they were feeling. They were crying and holding up pictures and big pieces of paper that said "I miss you." It made us really emotional. I thought: Oh my gosh, I'm so thankful that I'm still breathing. I'm still living. I still have my family. So many of those people lost their loved ones. But we also tried to bring them a little happiness. The song is emotional, but you don't want to make them even more sad than they already are. The concert in D.C. was the night after the New York concert and it was a little more upbeat. In New York the people were sad and nervous, so we sang "The Gospel Medley" and "Emotions." In Washington we felt the strength and the energy from the crowd. It was a feeling of "We're going to make it through this!"

MICHELLE Both of the performances were emotion packed. We performed "Emotions" and then "Survivor" at the one in Washington—we had to let the world know that Americans are survivors, and that we are going to make it through this, and we can't let anybody stop us. It's a song that makes you want to work harder, love stronger, and appreciate life more. And of course we also did "The Gospel Medley" because gospel music always feeds and nurtures the soul. Most people turn to gospel or

God when they are in trouble and bad things happen. So it was cool that we could sing our gospel song and touch people.

In New York we did "Emotions" and "The Gospel Medley." I remember that I was kind of nervous going out onstage for some reason. But it was amazing to look out and see thousands of people who had decided to come out and see artists from Jay-Z to Billy Joel perform. I actually just bought the CD of the New York concert. I remember how cool it was when people in the crowd were getting with Jay-Z while he was rapping his "H to the Izzo" song. It was good to see New Yorkers smiling, laughing, and dancing—and to help take their minds off what had happened, if only for a few hours.

CONFE**ſſ**IONſ 21

BEYONCÉ My group has always been my biggest support system. I don't have many other close friends, and I never did. I guess that's because having a music career doesn't allow for much of a social life. Anyone who has two true friends in this life is very lucky. And if you have more than that, you are truly blessed. A friend is someone who loves you no matter what—they're happy for you and support you and care about your well-being. You need to be able to trust them, and earning that trust is hard. Some people can't handle it when their friends become successful. They are only comfortable when you are struggling. It's probably because they're just not happy with themselves. Instead of them trying to grow along with you, they want you out of their life. But that's how you find out who your real friends are. Fortunately, we've been sheltered from a lot of fake friends because of my parents. Nobody could take advantage of us, because my mom and dad wouldn't let him or her get to us. Really, my best friends are Kelly and Michelle and my family.

I guess one of the reasons I found the transition from singer to actress pretty easy is because when you are in the public eye like we are, you have to learn how to put on a show. Not only do we have to give a great performance onstage, but sometimes we have to perform offstage, too. When we're out in public at a show or a benefit, we can't let people know when we are down. Our fans came a long way and paid good money to see us, and they expect to get what they paid for. They don't want to see us depressed. And sometimes it's hard to hide those emotions.

When my uncle Jonny passed a few years ago, I found out about it in a store. Kelly and I were going shopping to buy coffee when my cell phone rang and I got the message. I was so upset, I went and sat down in a corner and cried. (You see, I was very close to him and he took care of me when I was little.) And as soon as I sat down, a fan came over and said, "Oh, my God! You're Beyoncé." And it was hard to act like nothing had happened. I had to pretend everything was okay and wipe the tears from my eyes, get on my feet, sign the autograph, and smile. For just a split second I thought, Will she understand if I say I need to be alone? But then again, what if she's a true fan and has always wanted to meet me and now is her only chance? She probably will never see me again, and I don't want to disappoint her.

There are a lot of situations like that, when you just want to be alone because you've had a terrible day or you're exhausted, but you still have to give 100 percent. Sometimes, when you have a few days like that in a row, by the fifth day, you feel like you can't take it anymore. And that's when being in the group helps, because there is another person there. In my case, there are two other people. And if I don't want to answer a question, they can answer it for me. Or, if I'm running on empty, they can prop me up and help me go on. We split everything three ways. I feel really bad for solo artists who have to take that pressure all by themselves.

NOBODY'S PERFECT

I have seen plenty of unflattering photos of myself— paparazzi shots of me walking through an airport after just waking up from a long flight. I'm not flawless. I try to be the best person I can be, but I'm not a physically perfect specimen. I hit bad notes. I gain weight on my thighs. I have bad hair days. I have bad fashion days, too. I'm human.

In person, I don't look as good as I do in my videos. That sometimes surprises fans. They see me somewhere with bags under my eyes and say, "Ew, she's got bags!" And they're not talking Louis Vuitton. They don't know that I had to finish a twenty-four-hour video shoot, and then I took the red-eye to perform a song at an awards show on another side of the world. Or someone will make a comment if I have a few zits across my forehead. Hey, I break out sometimes! It's the result of wearing full makeup, all day, every day, for two weeks straight when I'm at performances, sweating under hot lights. Sometimes I put on a few pounds—I can't always eat nutritiously. Then I hear remarks like, "Beyoncé got fat!" It's tough having to watch my weight. I'm twenty years old, and I don't want to watch what I eat at every meal, but it's a part of being a celebrity. I just try to keep my mind off it. I hired a personal trainer, and we work out a lot. And they have no-carb chocolate now, which is saving my life. So I have some of that, but it's still not like real chocolate. I just deal with it. I have one cheat day on Sundays. I eat whatever I want then. (I look forward to Sundays, that's my life! I'm going to write a song called "Wish Every Day Was Sunday.") Thankfully, most fans can see past things like that. They support me no matter what. And they are the reason why I work this hard.

THE REAL DEAL

Most commercial hits are simple songs—by simple I mean not too deep. Of course I'm not saying that all of them are simple. Sometimes you write a brilliant song, and it's so great that people can't help but like it. But most songs that stick in your head after the first listen are not that complex, and for that reason alone they do really well. Music critics don't always consider that to be real music. The way I see it, I think all music is real music.

I don't think anyone in this world has the right to criticize music that someone else makes, because it's a valid form of self-expression. It's art. If an artist is so consumed by an emotion that he or she responds by drawing some circles and a dot on a piece of paper, I can't judge their feelings and say whether that sketch is the best possible representation of what they feel. I think it's terrible for people to say what is and what is not real music. A song is subjective—you either respond to it or you don't, but you shouldn't disqualify it. Just because someone's song doesn't sound anything like mine, I can't say that it's not real. I'm sure that it's very real to the person or people who created it.

I feel like I can never make everyone happy. I want to satisfy the fans. I want to satisfy the critics. I want to satisfy my record label. I want to satisfy my parents. I want to satisfy Kelly and Michelle. Oh, and I want to satisfy myself. The problem is that all those people have different things that they find satisfying. It's impossible—absolutely impossible—to please them all. I want to sell records, but I also want those records to get good reviews. And unfortunately, nine times out of ten, those two don't go together. I don't know what the solution is. I feel like I can't do or say some of the things I want to because the business is so political. I try to find the happy medium, but think about it: There's nothing to be happy about if you're a medium. People expect my music to evolve, even though the sound I have is what made them like me in the first place. So I try out things that I wouldn't normally do, because I want to be different while still being true to myself.

NEVER ENOUGH

I'm never satisfied. I'm proud of that. It's easy to become comfortable with success. Sometimes people let that get to their heads and they become lazy. But I like to find new challenges and say, "Next I'm going to write all of the songs on my album. And I'm producing my own stuff." Then I get creative control of all aspects of my career, and critics cannot withhold the credit I deserve for that. To be as successful as we are at this age—writing our own music, choreographing our own routines, and thinking up our own video treatments—makes me very happy and proud, but I do not feel satisfied.

Next, I would like to try to write songs for other artists. I haven't been able to do that yet. I get too self-conscious. Every time I try, I agonize over every word. I'm like, No, that sounds dumb. They will hate that word. And that's something I have to overcome. I am very confident when I'm singing in the studio and onstage performing. I just have to learn how to carry that confidence over into songwriting before I try to write songs for other artists.

I have been approached to write songs for a few singers, but I'm not entirely ready for that pressure. And when I do write songs for people, I don't want to write for just anyone. It has to be someone I really admire. It would be hard to write and produce a song, and then just give it away. It would be like giving away a child. Before I let that song go, I have to make sure the person I'm giving it to can take care of it properly. I also think it's very important for performers to write their own material, because everyone's vocabulary is different. For instance, if I like something, I might say, "That's tight," whereas they would say, "That's good." Or they might say, "That sucks," and I would say, "That's wack." If they're singing a song, it should be written in their own words. Then the lyrics will be more personal. Everyone should value his or her own voice.

Not a Wild Child

KELLY I might seem wild, but I'm really sensitive, even though I can come across as a little joker. I can also be very moody when it comes to clothes. I think I'm going through a weird phase now, where I just wear little T-shirts or tank tops and jeans. I like to slip on flip-flops or a pair of cute tennis shoes (unless it's wintertime). Having a cool bag is important, too. Comfort is always my first consideration, but I don't want to look too comfortable. My look still has a little bit of ruckus to it, say, a pair of holey jeans. But the most important thing I carry with me is not anything in my closet. Well, I guess he can be found there sometimes. He's my dog.

I have a beautiful teacup Yorkie named Mohawk—he actually has a little Mohawk on his head—who won't stop chewing up my pillows. I don't know what I ever did without him. I talk to him all the time. When I decided that I wanted a dog and went pooch shopping, Beyoncé said, "This dog needs to be different." Because all the pets we've had have been absolutely nuts. We had a kitty named Master P, and he was just a straight-up thug—the most hard-core ghetto cat that you've ever seen in your life. This cat did not meow, he barked. We also had a rabbit named Asia, and she was nutty, too.

Mohawk is absolutely wild. I got him when he was only two months old. I wanted to make sure that he was healthy before I got too attached, because I had real bad luck with my previous two Yorkies. They both passed away on me. But Mohawk is definitely healthy. He's up at six o'clock in the morning, just barking his head off. He keeps me company. He's good company too, maybe even better than having a guy around. Although he acts just like a man. He always makes a mess and expects me to pick up after him. I've had him for nine months now, and I am in love with him. He comes with me everywhere—even the recording studio.

SPLIT PERSONALITY

MICHELLE Some people may not know that Tenitra is my real first name. That's what I've been called my entire life. Unless my mother was trying to get my attention—then I would hear: "Tenitra Michelle! Tenitra Michelle Williams!" So when I come home to Rockford, I'm Tenitra again.

The only people who call me Michelle are the people who know me as part of Destiny's Child. Even people who I meet more than once get to know me as Michelle, and then I tell them my real first name. Either way, I'm cool. I answer to both, so it doesn't matter what I'm called: Michelle, Tenitra, even my nickname TT. In a way, I feel like I'm two people.

I like going by two names because it helps keep my public and private lives separate, but mentally it can still be hard sometimes. Michelle is cool because that's my business name—a stage name. When I'm performing, even when I do interviews, I feel like I become this other person—Michelle. But then off camera and off duty, if I'm hanging out with my brother, somehow I switch back to Tenitra. At home when my friends call me up, they say, "Tenitra, what's up, girl? How you doing?"

The name-change suggestion came about in a meeting with record-company execs. They had lots of issues they wanted to discuss with me, from the image of the group to how much hard work it would require. The record company didn't know me at all, so for them to allow me to join this group, they really had lots of important points to get across. So by the time they got around to suggesting that they would prefer me to be known as Michelle instead of Tenitra, I was a little disappointed. They said, "We would like you to go by Michelle." And I wasn't exactly happy about it, but I wasn't about to pass up a once-in-a-lifetime oppor-tunity just because I couldn't be called Tenitra. "Are you sure, you know, that I can't go by Tenitra?" I asked. But then I just said, "Okay, what-ever you say." If getting into this group meant that I couldn't keep my first name, then I was willing to give it up for my middle name, Michelle.

The record company had already figured all this out before my audition, so to Beyoncé and Kelly, I have been Michelle since day one. I didn't want to make an issue about the name change, so I didn't even ask Mathew. And to this day we haven't even really discussed it. If that is what it took so that the group could move on with their dreams, then I was happy to help. I was not about to make things harder than they already were for Beyoncé and Kelly. After all they had done for me already, I wanted to be cooperative.

At first it was hard getting used to being called Michelle. I wouldn't answer, because I wasn't used to hear-ing it. Of course, now Beyoncé and Kelly know that I'm really Tenitra. I wasn't sure if it would bother my mom. Fortunately, she didn't make a big deal out of it. No matter what, I am her daughter. She gave me the name Michelle as a middle name, so it's still a part of me.

So I've grown used to being called Michelle. And I like the fact that I have Tenitra stories and then, after I joined Destiny's Child, I have Michelle stories—and yet somehow I'm the subject of both. When I put out my solo record, I will still be Michelle, just to keep it consistent.

MYSTERIOUS WAYS

I'm modest. No, you will not see me running around in a thong at the beach. If I am on vacation, I might wear a two-piece bikini, but I'll get a matching skirt or sarong to wrap around me. I'll never, ever take it off on the beach. I barely take it off when I get in the pool! I love my sarongs. I just could never walk in a bathing suit without it. That's just the kind of girl I am. I have never been a rebel. Going out into the world has opened my mind up a lot, and personally, I think that the body of a woman is sacred. It should remain a mystery to men. If you're showing everything off, then your mystery has been solved. This goes for men, too. I think it's better to leave a little something to the imagination. I am getting older now. In a few more years, I may be ready for marriage, and I want my body to remain a mystery to whomever I am with. I want my husband to be surprised and excited about what I'm working with. I could be wearing some hiphugger jeans and a tank top, but I'm still somewhat of a mystery. So I choose to be sexy but still covered up and classy.

STAYING GROUNDED

I don't hang out with many people who are in the industry. I keep in touch with the members of 112. Lance Bass two-ways me every now and then, and I'll two-way him back sometimes. Since we all travel constantly, it's hard not to run into other groups while we're all touring. One day we bumped into 'N Sync in Germany, and a week later we saw them again in Japan. Later, Lance sent me a message that said, "You can't escape us, Michelle!" That was his way of saying we all work too much.

We're always at the same awards shows, even when they're halfway around the globe. It's nice to run into people you know when you're on the road, so whenever we do see one another, we try to have fun when we can.

But the majority of my friends are either in my hometown or in Chicago. They help to keep me grounded. They say things like, "Look, girl, I knew you when you was asking me for lunch money at school, you know what I'm saying?" I really don't want to just have a two-way-pager relationship with a celebrity. I think that's so Hollywood. I mean, why can't we talk to each other on the phone every now and then? It takes the same amount of time to two-way as it takes you to pick up the phone and say, "Hey, what's up?" A two-way relationship can be real artificial, so I don't really get into asking celebrities for their two-way numbers. That's just not a real conversation.

When you become a celebrity, people expect you to be perfect. They want you to have it all together—no flaws— but the reality is that no one is ever perfect. We still make mistakes, but we have been able to learn from them. We got booed when we performed for the 2001 NBA finals. At the time, we thought it would be cute to decorate the L.A. Lakers and 76ers outfits—kind of girly them up a little bit. Kelly had on a 76ers top, Beyoncé wore an NBA jersey that had L.A. on it, and I wore a Lakers shirt. That really pissed people off. Then again, the 76ers were losing, so that might have had something to do with the crowd's response. So East Coast people were just trying to be loyal to their team. It's not that the crowd was unhappy with our performance.

We were trying to be equal and not show any favoritism to one team. We were trying to please everybody. Now we've learned: You can never please all of the people all of the time. Next time if we get another chance to do something like that, we'll just wear regular clothes.

THE "BREAKUP"?

KELLY Two thousand and one has been Destiny's Child's year. It was incredible from start to finish. Beyoncé, Michelle, and I are so proud of the fact that we got a chance to take home not one, not two, but five Billboard Awards. And we won Billboard's Artist of the Year trophy for the second year in a row, which has never happened before. That is a groundbreaking achievement. And the great thing about the Billboard Awards is that they are based on facts—record sales and radio airplay—and not on the opinion of biased critics. But instead of the media focusing on our achievements, they had to say something negative about Destiny's Child. Unfortunately, the story they decided to tell was a lie. By misquoting Beyoncé, presumably reporters had hoped to put fear inside Michelle and me and make us nervous. But we are still right here by Beyoncé's side. We're not going anywhere.

BEYONCÉ The day after the 2001 Billboard Awards there were crazy rumors flying around. We actually made headlines—"Destiny's Child Split," "Destiny's Child on the Shelf," "Destiny's Child

Breakup," "Destiny's Child Going Separate Ways." And that was just the newspapers and Internet. I have been out of touch with TV and radio, so I don't know exactly what they were saying, but from what I've heard, it was all lies. Essentially, the media claimed I said that Destiny's Child needed a break from one another. They made it sound as if I wanted to get away from Kelly and Michelle because we couldn't stand to be near one another anymore.

Well, I never even said that Kelly, Michelle, and I needed a break from one another. What I said was that we needed a break from the media—from being out there in the public eye—and this is a perfect example that explains why. Destiny's Child is more than a full-time job, it's a twenty-four-seven lifestyle, and it can be exhausting. We have been out and about for nearly three years nonstop. We desperately need a rest from the public and the world. And during that break we are going to work on solo projects, then we will come back and do more Destiny's Child records. But irresponsible reporters left out the part of the quote that said we were going to come back together. And then newspapers all over the country—and, for all I know, around the world—picked up that quote, and it snowballed into an avalanche of rumors.

Before I realized what had happened, we were buried in speculation and lies. Kelly and I are like sisters. We have lived under the same roof for ten years. Nothing and no one could ever keep us apart. And we love Michelle—we would not be complete without her. And even though we don't see her every day, she is always in our hearts, on our minds, and on our speed dial. Destiny's Child's breakup is not going to happen anytime soon. And someday after we do stop performing, we will still be friends and one day will come together for Destiny's Child reunion tour.

MICHELLE I may live in Chicago and not in Houston with Kelly and Beyoncé, but we are as tight as three unrelated people could possibly be. I almost feel like we've been in an elevator together for the past three years—and the elevator ride has gone straight up, up, up. Sure, there have been some downs and bumps along the way, but they only brought us closer together.

We are in no way running away from one another.

Oprah's On

BEYONCÉ Of course winning the Billboard Artist of the Year Award was a great accomplishment for us, but what was even more exciting was our appearance on *Oprah,* which followed. We were so happy to be on the show. Talk about an independent woman! Oprah is the greatest. We have always looked up to her.

It was the third week in December, just a few days before Christmas, when we took the red-eye to Chicago to tape the show. Now, everyone knows that Oprah is one of the nicest women in the world, but I just want to say that her staff is equally as warm. The entire time we worked with them, they were kind, helpful, and very professional. We had a blast.

We were on with Charlotte Church, a young soprano, and Nancy Wilson, the famous jazz singer. They are both incredibly talented artists, and it was wonderful to share the segment with them. We were asked to perform two songs off our Christmas album. We came out singing "The Eight Days of Christmas." The crowd was on their feet, clapping and singing—even Oprah sang along. We were wearing these beautiful formfitting, knee-length white dresses with white lace accents and rhinestones. Oprah loved them. After we finished the song, she gave props to my mom for all the wonderful outfits she creates for us, and to my dad for being a great manager, and she said hi to Michelle's mom, who drove in for the taping. She complimented us for being great role models, because we don't smoke, drink, or swear. We were so flattered.

It was great talking with her because it gave us a chance to clear up any rumors about our breaking up. We let everyone watching know that we are still very much together, but after putting out four albums in four years, we needed a break from being in public. We talked a little bit about our upcoming solo projects, and said that Destiny's Child would still be appearing together over the coming years. After all, we were going on an international tour four months after that show.

We've always felt very lucky to share a makeup artist, Reggie Wells, with Oprah. But being on her show was a dream come true.

ʃolo but ∩ot ʃo Long

MICHELLE I can see all of the lights of downtown Chicago from the window of my hotel room. I'm staying here to be near the recording studio, because I'm hard at work on my solo album—that's my baby. I want to explore a different sound. The music is relaxed and comfortable in the style of old-school Motown. I want my songs to dig deep into the hearts and minds of people and into their souls. I want to get away from the new pop-R&B sound, because I grew up in an old-school household. I was raised on Al Green and Aretha. The only new CD I bought recently was Jill Scott, and she sounds like a jazz singer from the seventies. Other than Jill, I've been listening to America and stuff from that era—everything from the Bee Gees to Marvin Gaye. My hope is that a live band will be able to play all the songs on my album. I love the sound of live musicians. I know that it can't sound too old school because of my fan base, but at the same time, I've got to do what I want to do.

I'm collaborating with my brother, Erron, on my album. I had a writer help out with the lyrics, and Kayla Parker is my vocal producer. But my brother is producing the music tracks. He's great to work with. It's magical: We have so much fun and it's stress free. In the studio, I listen to him and I try not to look at him as my brother—I respect him as a producer. He knows what he wants the songs to sound like. He's driven and determined to be successful, and he's not going to let anything stop him. I'm excited for him. Hopefully he'll get lots of work after people hear the songs he has done on my album.

I'm cowriting most of the songs. I'm good at coming up with melodies for the chorus. Verses are hard because they have to be structured, and I'm still learning how to do that. As for the lyrics? Basically, I ask God to speak to me. When I was working on "I Heard a Word" with the song's producers, Buster and Shavoni, God spoke to me. Basically He said, "Girl, you will be fine. What are you worried about? You know everything is going to be okay because I have you in My hands." If you acknowledge God, He will give you direction—you just have to seek Him out. There's a proverb that says, "In all thy ways acknowledge God, and He will direct your path." And I believe in that. I had young people in mind when I cowrote "I Heard a Word." They might think that in order to communicate with God, they need to go to a church and get down on their knees and pray. But you could be driving your car in traffic and still talk to God. He's your friend. He will ride shotgun with you!

I recorded another song called "Everything Is Going to Be Okay." It's upbeat, light and fluffy, but really groovy.

I want to encourage people. That's why I want this album to be contemporary inspirational. It can't be categorized as gospel, because gospel can be narrow-minded, even though the word "gospel" means truth—good news. I guess that in a way my album could be considered gospel. After all, I am going to tell the truth, and that's good news! But from a marketing standpoint, I don't want to be limited to just gospel. I want my songs to be played on R&B, pop, and contemporary Christian stations—and all of the other radio stations, too. I just don't want to cater to one crowd. I need to appeal to all kinds of people, because no matter what your religion is—even if you think that you don't have any—you still need to be uplifted. We all need inspiration, now more than ever.

The cool thing about choosing to do inspirational music is that I can feel the power of God behind my voice, and people can feel it when I'm singing. That's not some trick that a producer can duplicate in a recording studio.

I will be sporting a much different look when I come out with videos to support my solo album. In other words: You can say good-bye to my belly button and thighs for a while. I plan to be a bit more covered up—leather jackets and long trench coats, maybe a funky turtleneck and some heels. That's more my style. I especially like hats. I don't wear them all that much in the group, but Kangol caps are my favorite. A Kangol helps to rock an outfit.

BACK TO SCHOOL

There's still so much that I want to do. I want my college degree, and someday I am going to get it. I'll return to Illinois State University to finish it. I've already started to pay back my student loans. All my money goes to the U.S. Department of Education! No flashy bling-bling for me. So yes, even though I have two Grammys, I still want to go back to college. Maybe I'll graduate and end up in the criminal-justice field.

Somebody was telling me that I would never want to take a nine-to-five job after being in Destiny's Child. And I said, "You don't know what I would want out of life." Because I can see myself doing precisely that. I mean, I might have to be my own boss, because I don't know if I could handle a boss working over me. I definitely wouldn't want to be anyone's employee—after all, I am an independent woman.

Someday I want to get married and have children. I'm hoping to have twins, because twins run really deep in my family. I would like to be married by age twenty-six or twenty-seven and then maybe have my first child by the time I'm thirty.

Look Out, Lenny

KELLY I feel like I have this whole big house to myself. Once in a while I can hear Solange singing, but she hasn't been around much now that she's busy auditioning dancers for her own act. It's so quiet around here with Beyoncé gone. She took most of her stuff with her—she even packed up our "pillow room," so now if I ran down the hall and jumped in there, I'd land flat on the hardwood floor instead of on hundreds of fluffy cushions. But the peace and quiet gives me time to think about the kind of sound I want on my solo album—I plan to make a lot of noise.

Gospel is something that I will want to explore, but the world needs to get in touch with a new side of Kelly—my inner rock chick. I imagine that I will probably do at least one gospel song on my album, but the rest of it will be rock 'n' roll. Rock with kind of a twist of R&B. I want to be like a female Lenny Kravitz, even though I can't play the guitar. I was learning how to play the bass. I really need to get some more lessons, because I think it would be cool to be a bass player. As far as the lyrics are concerned, I want to really talk about life. I don't just want to write about my own experiences, though. I want to give my take on everything that's going on in the world today. I want to talk about love. I want to talk about my dog, Mohawk. I don't care what the subject is, as long as I flip it the right way and make the beat hot, then I can promise that you are gonna love it.

I hope that my album helps people to understand me and see where I'm coming from. There are still a lot of people who do not know much about me, and if they have not found out yet, they are gonna know when they hear this CD. I have been inspired a lot by Lenny's new album. He has a song called "God Save Us All," and we can all relate to that sentiment—especially after the 9/11 attacks. But I also want to listen to a lot of older rock songs and try to bring that sound back—but in a modern way. I need to take a trip to the record store and do a lot of looking and listening. I want to buy music from the sixties, the seventies, and, of course, the eighties. Sweet dreams are made of that music.

TV STAR

I recently got a cameo appearance on *The Hughleys*. That one cameo led to three more appearances. I play D. L. Hughley's niece. He hasn't seen her since she was three, and she just pops up. She's very free spirited, and she hasn't had any type of direction in her life. Basically, she's all on her own. She hasn't had any direction from her parents, so she travels the country by herself—she's an aspiring music star. She ends up in L.A., and of course that's where her uncle Daryl lives. That's where she's been trying to get anyway, because she feels that's the happening place in terms of the record companies and making connections.

The biggest challenge of this part is acting, period. I have to play a character I can only kind of relate to. I've been very blessed to have three parents; she doesn't have anybody. She says things like, "I haven't heard from my father in so long, I don't care what I call him." She isn't being mean—she really just doesn't care. Her outlook doesn't affect her, but it affects her family in the end. They see that she doesn't know any better. She takes D. L. Hughley's daughter to get a belly-ring piercing! She doesn't have any direction from adults, and I was very lucky that I did.

Stayed tuned, who knows what lies ahead—maybe even more appearances on the show.

In the future I would like a shot at doing a film or another TV show. There is not one particular type of role that I am interested in; I would just like to pursue acting. Two of my favorite actresses are Angela Bassett and Julia Roberts. I love Angela because her acting style is so incredible. Her facial expressions are subtle, but you always know what her characters are feeling. She makes every situation she gets in believable. There are a lot of actresses who cannot manage to do that. As far as Julia is concerned, I like how she can be serious and funny at the same time. I love her radiant smile. There is nothing else like it in Hollywood. Acting appeals to me in a way that is totally different from singing and dancing. I think it would be fascinating to explore another character that is the opposite of me. That would be a huge challenge.

Of course, I got the idea from talking to Beyoncé when she started preparing to film *Austin Powers 3*. I remember when she came home to Houston after she finished filming *Carmen* in Los Angeles. It was difficult for her to play Carmen, but she really got into the character. She was sizzling in every scene. I'm curious about the challenge acting offers—trying to inhabit another character and seeing if you can pull it off convincingly. Currently she's in the process of transforming into Foxxy Cleopatra. But she says it's fun, even though I can see that it is a lot of work. I had fun visiting her on the set. I am glad that she gets to do comedy this time—that girl has a beautiful laugh. And I know she must like hearing people call her Foxxy. She is one foxy lady, that's for sure.

ROCKIN' OUT

I think that my interest in acting is similar to why I want to rock out on my album—it's a change of pace. I want to be known as someone other than an R&B singer. I'm sure that a lot of people would be shocked to see me strumming a bass, jamming, maybe kicking over an amp onstage. But traditional rock 'n' roll has changed. Now most rock songs that you hear on the radio are considered pop, except for the really hard rock bands like Creed and Incubus. I love loud guitars. Beyoncé and I used to ride around in her truck, which was her first car. We used to cruise around and search all over the dial for this song by the Cardigans called "Love Fool"—we loved the way rock music made us feel. It's great driving music. I would let my hair blow in the wind and put my arms out the window like I was flying. That's why I love rock. I would say that R&B has a bit more soul—I'm not saying that rock doesn't have any soul, but it's just got that edgier quality to it. R&B is sexier, though. There are definitely some rock songs that are so sexy, of course. To this day, one of my favorites has to be the Goo Goo Dolls' "Iris." That song is so tight! It's such an incredible track. I also like Sarah McLachlan—"In the Arms of an Angel" and "Ice Cream." I can relate to the lyrics of that one: "Your love is better than ice cream, better than anything else that I've tried." And then there's Sheryl Crow. I love her, too. I may not look like a typical rock star, but I do think the red hair helps.

Yeah, Baby!

BEYONCÉ Out here in Hollywood, I feel like I'm starting life all over again! I'm getting the chance to film another movie, and this one will appear on the big screen—*Austin Powers 3*. Slowly but surely, I am adjusting to the L.A. lifestyle. I love the cute apartment I found on the outskirts of Beverly Hills—it feels more like home than a hotel room. Now if I can only find a new car that I like. Los Angeles reminds me more of home than New York—this city's all spread out and the only place people walk is on treadmills at the gym. You need wheels if you want to get around. Of course, this is a little fancier than Houston—here it seems like they always have valets to park your car for you. Even at Burger King!

Auditioning for *Austin Powers 3* was very cool—even though I was not. I still don't feel really confident about acting, because the only other movie I've done was *Carmen: The Hip-Hopera*. Every *Carmen* review I read mentioned something good about my performance, which was refreshing. So seeing all those glowing reviews of *Carmen* reassured me. Although there is so much that I need to learn, even with the lingo and the slang I hear on the set, I have no idea what film people are talking about half the time. So that can be intimidating, to say the least.

I was not my usual calm self at the *Austin Powers 3* audition. The environment didn't help at all—the office was stuffy and the lights were too bright. It was uptight and intense. It hardly helped to make me feel shagadelic. My heart was beating fast, my mouth was dry, my palms were clammy—I had to wipe my hands on my pants before I shook hands with Mike Myers. But Mike is a real gentleman. He made me feel very comfortable. He never stops doing impressions and telling jokes. He was so funny that he broke the ice with the producer and director. I actually got to audition directly with him.

The first time was just an informal meeting. It was me; my mother; Mike; the director, Jay Roach; and the producer. I didn't have a script, so the pressure wasn't that severe. The second time a casting agent gave me the script, and I read a bit of it with Mike: "Well, hello, Austin Powers. My name is Foxxy Cleopatra—and I'm a whole lotta woman!" He giggled when I said that line, so I knew that had to be a good sign. Then he put up his hands to shield his face. He said, "You are so beautiful, I can barely look at you. I must turn around now." All I could say was, "Oh, Lord. I can't believe I'm doing this." Mike pretended like he was nervous too, which I know he wasn't. He said things like, "I'm completely socially awkward, you know. And I don't know how to— I actually have no idea how to do this scene." He was just trying to ease the tension for me. And it worked. I relaxed a little bit.

I knew that I would be really lucky if I got this movie role, but if I didn't, that would be fine, too. It's not like I didn't have a music career to fall back on. Thank goodness I had my mama with me. If my mom hadn't been there, I don't know what I would have done. I might have been too intimidated to speak. I was scared that I was going to say the wrong thing and ruin it, so I thought it would be best if I listened and didn't say much. My mom did all the talking—

fortunately she's a real charmer, and she did everything but read my lines for me!

Of course, I did say something that I instantly regretted. "How do you feel about doing a comedy?" the producer asked me. The right response would have been "I'd love to!" Unfortunately, I'm just a really honest person, even when I shouldn't be, so I said, "Well, I love comedy, but I don't know if I'm all that funny. I don't know if I could make people laugh. But I would like to try." That's probably not what you should tell a Hollywood producer who is thinking about casting you in their multimillion-dollar comedy. But obviously, it didn't knock me out of the running. I still got the part in the end. Maybe they found my sincerity and honesty refreshing. The next day, my agency called and said, "Beyoncé, I think you got the movie!" And all I could say was "Oh my God!"

Even after *Carmen*, I never expected that I would be offered a part in a big-budget Hollywood blockbuster, let alone a major franchise like Austin Powers. It's going to be a huge summer movie, and I'm the leading lady, an international woman of mystery! As an actor, I get to follow in the footsteps of Elizabeth Hurley and Heather Graham, and as a musician, I get to follow Madonna's lead—she sang "Beautiful Stranger" in the second movie. I get to sing the title track of this movie. It's such a great opportunity for me, and everybody has been really nice, and not fake nice.

I met with the makeup artist, whose job is to make me look, well, foxy, and I got to say hi to all the characters— Mini-Me is especially adorable—and we've started rehearsing together. I'm starting to feel more confident and comfortable. Overall, it's been a fun learning experience. Maybe I'll get my own Mini-Beyoncé!

In *Austin Powers 3*, I play another very sexy character, but at least she's sweeter than Carmen—she's Austin's sidekick, not Dr. Evil's. Some of my costumes are so slinky that they barely qualify as costumes. I'm playing a cross between

Foxy Brown (Pam Grier's famous movie character, not to be confused with the rapper) and Cleopatra Jones. Mike's character is a swinger from the sixties, but I'm straight outta the seventies. I talk real tough, just like the women in the black films from that era. I can relate a lot to her, because she's really strong and sassy and she has got a lot of soul. She's supposed to be over the top and exaggerated, sort of a caricature, which gives me license to overact. Getting to do scenes with Mike is such a treat, because he's a comedic genius. We have good chemistry together. Maybe I can learn some of his tricks by the end of the movie. At the very least he can teach me how to tell a joke.

The hardest thing about making this movie has been remembering the lines (actually, working out with a personal trainer and watching what I eat is no picnic, either). As it is, I have a tough time recalling the lyrics to songs that I've written myself, even after singing them hundreds of times! Now I have to remember the exact words from a script I only got a few weeks ago, while also kicking down a door and pulling out a gun on the bad guy. I also have to make sure that I'm standing in the correct spot, and then I need to count how many steps I'm supposed to take to hit my next mark, where a camera is already positioned to film me. So far so good, though. I like being able to kick butt and still look foxy. I feel like one of Charlie's Angels!

Another reason I was so uneasy at the audition was that I was worried the producer and the director might have preconceived notions about me being some kind of diva. And I was so afraid what the press would write when word got out. I was expecting to see items like: "Beyoncé's trying to act now. She must think she's Meryl Streep." That's why I didn't know if I wanted to do movies yet, because it seems like such a predictable move for a singer. And only once in a while do they turn out to be excellent. I knew that it was going to be an uphill battle. But I was ready for the challenge. I knew I'd have to work extra hard and be especially good if I wanted to be taken seriously and accepted by the other full-time actors—the negative stereotypes are so pervasive.

Even Cher had a hard time breaking into movies, and she's Cher! I was watching this special about her on TV. She was talking about her own struggles in Hollywood. She said she remembers audiences laughing when her name aired during the trailer for *Silkwood*. People didn't want to give her credit until they saw her performance in that movie, and she did an excellent job.

If you're a singer, people just don't want to give you a chance to prove that you can do anything else. Take Mariah, for example. She delivered a wonderful performance in her movie *Glitter*, but people don't want to give her props, even though she was going through a bad time in her life. I'm not Roger Ebert, but personally I think she did really well. Mariah, you get two very enthusiastic thumbs-up from me! Way before that, Diana Ross was incredible in *Mahogany*. People just want to scare you away from trying something new. Granted, it's worked to a certain extent, but not enough to stop me from taking a chance. Any kind of performance will help me to further develop my skills as an entertainer. This role will help me learn about myself, too. The more I learn, the more I grow as a person and as an artist.

It's ironic that I'm playing a character from the decade before I was born, but I do have a lot of favorite films from the seventies. I especially love *Cooley High* and *Sparkle*. The plots were cool, the lines were funny, and I liked the fashions and the music. I even identify with the story line of *Sparkle* because it was about three girls trying to get a record deal, and I could certainly relate to their struggles. *Cooley High* was just one of my mom's favorite movies, and she and I always loved watching it together. It's about a black high school in the sixties, and is both hilarious and sad.

I think the seventies were real cool—the clothes, the funk, the jive talkin'. And now, in a sense, I get to experience that for myself in this movie. The seventies get a bad rap. It wasn't all about sex, drugs, and disco. So much really powerful music comes from that era, and young people were more socially conscious. Kids weren't embarrassed to listen to songs like "Shining Star" that dealt with the subject of self-esteem. It was considered cool, not corny. People celebrated their race and they were proud to be black or whatever their background was. I may have an idealized impression of the time, but to me it seems like everyone was a lot more free back then. Teenagers were a lot more socially aware and active—they didn't just sit around watching *The Real World*.

Bring on the Funk

Coincidentally, "Shining Star," a song that I have always loved, is going to be in *Austin Powers 3*. I want to bring that same funky type of sound back for my solo album. I want to do a 2002 updated version of that live instrumentation. Back then people had a more open mind. They liked to hear everything from horns to full-on orchestras. And jazz was so popular—it influenced so many other different types of music. Black people, white people, all different races, were grooving to the same beat. Music was mixed up in the best possible way. Those songs had heart as well as soul—they're timeless. I think people will forever be listening to the music from back in the seventies. It sounds way more progressive than dated. That's the kind of praise I hope to get for my solo album.

My record will showcase me growing from a young lady into a woman. I'll be twenty-one when it comes out. Right now I'm trying to write a lot of love songs. I have always tried to keep my personal life separate, but I've been through relationships. I have experienced love and heartbreak, and I want to sing about it. I want a timeless record filled with love songs. I want to continue to write classic songs that people will be hearing for the rest of their lives—and then some. That's always my goal.

I make commercial music, because I want to grab the attention of everyday people. I want Destiny's Child to become a legendary group. But maybe someday I'll want to make an album where I don't think about anybody but myself. I just want to write what I'm feeling inside. I don't know if radio programmers would be interested in that, though.

Destiny's Child 2003

KELLY We don't know now what our next album will sound like—we want to surprise ourselves. Basically it will be a more mature Destiny's Child, both in terms of our sound and lyrics. By then we'll be older, and hopefully we'll have had some dating experiences—or possibly even boyfriends! But I seriously doubt it, as busy as we are now. At any rate, we'll have more to talk about then. As far as the sound, now that everybody is doing their own style and their own album, that's going to show on the future Destiny's Child album. And people are going to respect that, the fact that everybody has all their creative juices flowing. I'm still figuring out how to do my album, so I'm constantly asking Beyoncé questions. She's so wise. It's great that she will always give me advice. It's a blessing to me.

BEYONCÉ In the time leading up to the next album we record as Destiny's Child, I know for a fact that everybody is going to grow. On our next album there will be more collaboration, because these solo projects are helping us all become stronger songwriters and performers. Kelly and Michelle are so shy. When I try to write songs with them, they don't have much to say— I don't know why. Even if on the new album they don't want to write songs themselves (not everyone likes writing), they will have had new experiences to help us come up with new concepts. It will be interesting to hear gospel, rock, and soul sounds put together.

APPENDIXES

BEHIND THE MUSIC

ONSTAGE: 2001 *BILLBOARD* MUSIC AWARDS ARTIST OF THE YEAR AWARD.

Emcee Bernie Mac: Ladies and gentlemen, Sting!

Sting (Presenter): Good evening. Okay, this is *Billboard*'s Artist of the Year category, and one thing is certain about all of the finalists tonight: They all had a really good year! [Acknowledging a screaming fan in the audience] Darling, please, I'm working. We've been celebrating tonight number one songs and artists of rap, hip-hop, country, rock, reggae, blues, and pop, but now it's time to reveal the one artist who stands above all categories in a class by themselves: the artist you made number one by listening to, requesting their songs on the radio, and buying their CDs.

Announcer: Jennifer Lopez! Nelly! Destiny's Child! Shaggy!

Sting: And the Artist of the Year is … Destiny's Child!

Announcer: Destiny's Child collects five *Billboard* Music Awards. They are also the Duo/Group Artists, the Hot 100 Singles Artists, the Hot 100 Singles Duo/Group of the Year, and their single "Independent Women Part 1," featured in the movie *Charlie's Angels,* is the Soundtrack Single of the Year.

Kelly: Oh, oh, oh! I love you!

Michelle: I love you!

Kelly: Okay, we'll all calm down for real. Whew! Whew!

Michelle: Thank you!

Kelly: This means so much to us. Thank you so much, God, for just blessing us—thank you for surrounding us with wonderful people. Thank you, Jesus. We would also like to thank *Billboard* for supporting Destiny's Child; our label, Columbia Records/Sony. Donny Ienner, Tommy Mottola—thank you so much. Music World; Mathew, thank you so much for your vision. Thank you for believing in us. We love you so much!

Beyoncé: We love you, Daddy!

Kelly: Tina Knowles, our stylist—don't we look good, y'all? Thank you! No, for real. Okay? Our attorneys: Ken Hertz, Jonathan, thank you so much. Uh, who else? Wilhelmina, Hasbro, L'Oréal, Candie's—thank you so much!

Beyoncé: Tommy and Donny, thank y'all!

Kelly: Sure 'nough, sure 'nough!

Beyoncé: Yes!

Michelle: Yvette! Reggie! Ty! Angie! Everybody! The fans!

Beyoncé: God bless y'all!

Michelle: God bless you!

Bernie Mac: Now, you know what, ladies and gentlemen? Say all right! You all gotta give a warm applause to Destiny's Child: twenty years old! They came a long way on "Bootylicious"! And they say a mind is a terrible thing to waste—but a booty is, too!

◯ BACKSTAGE: IN THE PRESS ROOM

Announcer: Ladies and gentlemen of the press, I now present to you the winners of five *Billboard* Music Awards: Destiny's Child.

Journalist: So how do you girls feel?

Kelly: Winning a *Billboard* Award for Artist of the Year twice in a row? That is just amazing. Last year we won the award and it was an incredible event, and once again we had another beautiful year. It's the perfect way to end the year. But also, it really surprised us. It's unbelievable.

Journalist: So what can we expect from your next album?

Beyoncé: Well, you can expect a lot of excitement and new creativity! Because at that time all of Destiny's Child's solo records will have been released. Michelle is actually working on her solo record right now and mine will be coming up at the beginning of next year. Kelly's will be out at the end of next year.

Journalist: Are you guys staying home for the holidays?

Beyoncé: No, I'm actually going to be doing *Austin Powers 3,* the movie, but hopefully they'll give us a couple of days off the set.

Journalist: How do you like to celebrate the holidays?

Beyoncé: Family. Home. And food.

Kelly: Food!

Michelle: Food, yes. Absolutely.

Journalist: Any New Year's resolutions so far?

Beyoncé: Oh, gosh. Just to keep working hard.

Journalist: When's the movie coming out, the new *Austin Powers*?

Beyoncé: I'm actually not sure when it's coming out, but...

Publicist: July twenty-sixth!

Beyoncé: July twenty-sixth, okay. I need to remember that.

Journalist: Are you prepared for Mike Myers?

Beyoncé: He's hilarious and so nice, too. I expected him to be a lot jokier all the time—he did crack jokes and he was funny, but he was also really professional. I know when it gets late I'm not going to be able to say my lines, because I'm going to be laughing too hard.

Journalist: Say, "Yeah, baby!"

Beyoncé: Um, okay. "Yeeeeeeah, baby!"

Journalist: What are you wearing tonight?

Beyoncé: Cool shoes and an uncomfortable dress—there's no slit in it and my knees have been stuck together all night, and they're rubbing against each other. I can barely walk in this outfit. We won the award and I was happy, but then when we got to the foot of the staircase, I was like, Okay, now what am I going to do?

Journalist: Ain't fashion painful?

Beyoncé: It is tonight, but, you know, it's worth it. Yes, it's always worth it.

Journalist: Are you guys going to sing on each other's albums?

Kelly: Yes, definitely!

Journalist: Why are you doing solo albums?

Beyoncé: As Destiny's Child, we've put out four records in four years, and I know we need a break. We have worked really, really hard. And during the break, all the things that we always wanted to do individually, we'll do that. The great thing about Destiny's Child is that there's so much support in the group—everything that we do, we talk about and make sure that it fits Destiny's Child's agenda. That's our very first priority. And I know Michelle has always wanted to do a gospel record. Kelly has always wanted to do an alternative record. I always wanted to do like an old-school soul record. So now we can do that.

Journalist: There have been rumors that you guys talked about doing something with En Vogue?

Beyoncé: Yes, hopefully that can happen.

Kelly: That would be absolutely amazing. And the ladies were so nice, when we told them about it they were like, Of course!

Michelle: We were going to do Jay Leno together, but it got canceled.

Journalist: You guys are also known for your style as well. You guys come really dressed up all the time. I mean, I know your mother styles you, but what about you guys—who do you like? Whose style would you say, today, that you most admire? Like what artist out there?

Michelle: Janet!

Beyoncé: Janet, definitely.

Kelly: Yes, I would have to say Janet, too.

Journalist: What does Destiny's Child think about love? What's the secret to finding love?

Kelly: Love potion number nine!

Michelle: Before you can love anybody else you've got to love yourself.

Beyoncé: Yes, you have to love yourself first!

Kelly: And your band mates.

Announcer: Okay, this next question will have to be the last one—we've got to wrap this up.

Journalist: Do you have any tours coming to Finland?

Beyoncé: We'll be everywhere in Europe from April to July. So we'll see you there!

Announcer: Thank you very much, everyone.

◯ IN THE LIMO: BACK TO THE HOTEL

Michelle: Girls, my feet are killing me. I think I'm gonna need y'all to carry me up to my hotel room.

Beyoncé: I can't wait to get out of this dress and get into bed. I had to stick a piece of paper between my knees at one point. My legs were rubbing together all night. I was afraid a fire was going to start down there.

Kelly: Isn't it cool that Sting told us congratulations? He was looking good! Oh, I just got a two-way from Lance Bass. I don't know about you two, but this girl is gonna go out tonight and celebrate!

Michelle: Unh-uh. I have to be up at five A.M. to catch my flight. That's in like four hours.

Beyoncé: You go and have fun, Kelly. I'm gonna have a private party with my pillow, my blanket, and my remote control. That's my idea of a good time.

LIFE LESSONS
FROM DESTINY'S CHILD

1. Never give up—that's the key to being a survivor.

2. Don't hate the people who do something better than you—learn from their success.

3. Be thankful for challenges, they help you grow.

4. Don't dis anybody—negativity will only get in the way of your success.

5. Have faith in God. He is your friend and will help you through anything.

6. Don't let guys get up in your business. Be an independent woman.

7. A true friend is someone who sticks by you and offers you support, not drama.

8. Keep learning new skills—focusing your energy on something positive will help keep you out of trouble.

9. It's okay to look cute, but learn the difference between nice and nasty.

10. Cherish your life, your friends, and your family, and always thank God for your blessings.

ALL-TIME FAVORITE CDs

BEYONCÉ:
Shuggie's Boogie: Shuggie Otis Plays the Blues
Donny Hathaway: his greatest hits. All of them are good.
Aretha Franklin: her greatest hits—three different CDs' worth combined in one.
Michael Jackson: *Off the Wall* got reissued on CD. I've been listening to it every day. It's *still* hot.
Minnie Ripperton: her greatest hits

KELLY:
Sadé: any record!
Whitney Houston: her *Bodyguard* soundtrack
Kenny G: *Silhouette*
Michael Jackson: *Thriller*
Billy Joel: his greatest hits CD is absolutely amazing.

MICHELLE:
Yolanda Adams: *More Than a Melody, Mountain High Valley Low,* and *Believe*
Chicago: *Greatest Hits*
Carl Thomas: *Emotional*
Kurt Carr: *Awesome Wonder*
Jill Scott: both *Who Is Jill Scott?* and her live album. Jill Scott is an awesome singer and performer, and she has a wonderful spirit. I love her.

ALL-TIME FAVORITE
BIBLE QUOTES

BEYONCÉ One of my favorite passages is something we say in our church. It's from Phillipians 4:13: "I can do all things through Christ who strengthens me." I also like the passage we use in our show: "The invitation must be accepted, followed by appropriate conduct." It's not easy being a Christian and living your life right by God all the time—especially in the music industry. There is a lot of temptation. Even if you're not in this business, when you're growing up, it's a lot easier to do the wrong things. That line sums it all up. The invitation must be accepted—you have to want to take it—and then you have to follow it with appropriate behavior. Some people are only Christian when it's convenient, not all the time. (Mainly holidays.) I know I'm not perfect—everybody makes mistakes—but I try to be consistent even when it's not easy.

KELLY I have a favorite proverb from the Bible that I like to recite to myself—it keeps the success in perspective. It is Proverbs 20:15: "There is gold, and abundance of costly stones; but the lips informed by knowledge are a precious jewel." I always pray for knowledge. This passage stands out to me because it is so beautiful. It is saying that you might have all these material things around you, but the most important thing—the thing that really counts—is knowledge. It is like a priceless jewel. It is that special.

MICHELLE My favorite Bible passage is Proverbs 3:6: "In all your ways acknowledge him, and he will make straight your path." That's basically what I do all the time. I pray to God. I literally ask Him, "What do you want me to do?" As far as decisions I have to make, I want to put Him first and then He'll make sure that it all falls in line.

THE AWARDS

1998
Lady of Soul Awards, Best R&B/Soul or Rap New Artist for "No, No, No"

2000
Artist Direct (ADOMA) Awards, Favorite Group: Urban/Hip-Hop
Billboard Music Awards, Artist of the Year
Billboard Music Awards, Artist of the Year, Duo or Group
Billboard Music Awards, Hot 100 Singles Artist of the Year
Billboard Music Awards, Hot 100 Singles Artist of the Year, Duo or Group
Billboard Music Video Awards Nominees Maximum Vision Video for "Say My Name"
Billboard Music Video Awards Nominees Maximum Vision Video for Best R&B Clip of the Year for "Say My Name"
Grammy, Best R&B Performance by a Group or Duo with Vocal for "Say My Name"
Grammy, Best R&B Song for "Say My Name"
Lady of Soul Awards, R&B/Soul Album of the Year for *The Writing's on the Wall*
Lady of Soul Awards, Best R&B/Soul Single, Group, Band or Duo
MTV Video Music Awards, Best R&B Video for "Say My Name"
NAACP Image Awards, Outstanding Group or Duo for *The Writing's on the Wall*
Nickelodeon's Kid's Choice Awards, Favorite Singing Group
Soul Train Music Awards Sammy Davis Jr. Award—Entertainer of the Year

2001
American Music Awards, Favorite Band, Duo or Group—Soul/R&B
BET Awards, Female Group
Billboard Music Awards, Artist of the Year
Billboard Music Awards, Artist of the Year, Duo or Group
Billboard Music Awards, Hot 100 Singles Artist of the Year
Billboard Music Awards, Soundtrack Single Artist of the Year for "Independent Women Part 1"

Billboard Music Awards, Hot 100 Singles Artist of the Year, Duo or Group

BMI Pop Awards, Honored Most Performed BMI Songs for "Bills, Bills, Bills"

BMI Pop Awards, Honored Most Performed BMI Songs for "Say My Name"

MTV Music Video Awards, Best R&B Video for "Survivor"

Nickelodeon Kid's Choice Awards, Favorite Singing Group

NAACP Image Awards, Outstanding Group or Duo for "Survivor"

Teen Choice Awards, Choice Pop Group

Teen Choice Awards, R&B/Soul Album of the Year, Group, Band or Duo

2002

American Music Awards, Favorite Pop Album

American Music Awards, Favorite Soul Group

THE CONCERTS

We're not kidding when we say it's not easy being on the road. Here's a glimpse of what our tour schedule has looked like over the years—and this doesn't include all the interviews, award shows, radio station promotions, television appearances, and everything else it takes to get your name out there.

1999
October 28—Royal Oak, TX, Royal Oak Theatre
October 29—Boston, MA, Fleet Center
November 4—Atlanta, GA, The Tabernacle
October 27—TLC Tour
October 31—TLC Tour
November 2—TLC Tour
November 5—TLC Tour
November 7—TLC Tour
November 9—TLC Tour
November 12–13—TLC Tour
November 15—TLC Tour
November 18—TLC Tour
November 19—Toronto, Canada, Roy Thompson Hall
November 20—TLC Tour
November 22—TLC Tour
November 24—Indianapolis, IN, Conseco Fieldhouse

2000
February 12—San Francisco, CA, Hilton Towers
March 12—London, England, Shepherds Bush Empire
March 24—New York, NY, Madison Square Garden
March 26—Fairbanks, AK, University of Alaska
March 28—Anchorage, AK, The Egan
April 8—Lawrenceville, NJ, Alumni Gym at Rider University
April 10—Conway, AR, Farris Center
April 16—Amsterdam, Netherlands, Melkweg
April 17—Brussels, Belgium, Ancienne Belgique
April 18—Cologne, Germany, Live Music Hall
April 26—East Lansing, MI, Michigan State University
April 27—Athens, GA, Legion Field

April 28–29—Orlando, FL, Walt Disney World
May 5–6—Orlando, FL, Walt Disney World
May 7—Bakersfield, CA, Centennial Garden Arena
May 12—Orlando, FL, Walt Disney World
May 27—Quincy, IL, Oakley Civic Center
July 1—Arlington, TX, Six Flags Over Texas
July 2—Las Vegas, NV, The Joint
July 9—Dour, Belgium, Dour Festival
July 17—Tour of Australia
July 19—Tour of Australia
July 22—Vaughn, Canada, Paramount Canada's Wonderland
July 23—Rockford, IL, Davis Park
July 29—Houston, TX, Six Flags Astroworld
July 31—Bonner Springs, KS, Sandstone Amphitheatre
August 1—Maryland Heights, MO, Riverport Amphitheatre
August 4—Birmingham, AL, Birmingham Heritage
August 5—San Antonio, TX, Six Flags Fiesta Texas
August 6—Noblesville, IN, Deer Creek Music Center
August 7—Bethlehem, PA, The River Place
August 7—Antioch, TN, AmSouth Amphitheatre
August 8—Columbus, OH, Cooper Stadium
August 10—Sacramento, CA, ARCO Arena
August 11—Jackson, OR, Jackson County Fairgrounds
August 12—Valdosta, GA, Wild Adventures Theme Park
August 18—Oklahoma City, OK, Myriad Convention Center
August 19—Chicago, IL, United Center
August 21—Cincinnati, OH, Riverbend Music Center
August 23—Cleveland, OH, Gund Arena
August 24—Clarkson, MI, Pine Knob Music Theatre
August 26—Burgettstown, PA, Post Gazette Pavilion at Star Lake
August 30—Darien Center, NY, Darien Lake Performing Arts
    Center
August 31—Allentown, PA, Great Allentown Fair
September 1—Hartford, CT, Meadows Music Theater
September 6—Holmdel, NJ, PNC Bank Arts Center
September 8—Wantagh, NY, Jones Beach Amphitheatre
September 9—Mansfield, MA, Tweeter Center for the Performing
    Arts
September 11—Virginia Beach, VA, GTE Virginia Beach
September 13—Allegan, MI, Allegan County Fairgrounds
September 15—Camden, NJ, E-Center
September 16—Columbia, MD, Merriweather Post Pavilion
September 18—Charlotte, NC, Blockbuster Pavilion

September 20—Atlanta, GA, Lakewood Amphitheatre
September 22—Orlando, FL, Orlando Arena
September 23—Tampa, FL, Ice Palace
September 24—Huntsville, AL, Big Spring Jam
September 25—West Palm Beach, FL, Mars Music Amphitheater
September 27—New Orleans, LA, U.N.O. Lakefront Arena
September 29—Spring, TX, Cynthia Wood Mitchell Pavilion
September 30—Dallas, TX, State Fair of Texas
October 5—Denver, CO, Magness Arena
October 7—Little Rock, AR, Barton Coliseum
October 8—Phoenix, AZ, American West Area
October 10—Chula Vista, CA, Coors Amphitheatre
October 11–12—Universal City, CA, Universal Amphitheatre
October 14—Marysville, CA, Sacramento Valley Amphitheater
October 15—Concord, CA, Chronicle Pavilion at Concord
November 17—Manchester, England, Manchester Evening News
   Arena
November 18—London, England, London Arena
November 19—Birmingham, England, NEC Arena
November 21—Dublin, Ireland, The Point Theatre
December 8—Atlantic City, NJ, Mark G. Etess Arena
December 31—Los Angeles, CA, Staples Center Arena
December 31—San Jose, CA, San Jose State University

2001
February 8—San Antonio, TX, Freeman Coliseum
February 13—New York, NY, Hasbro Corporate Office
February 15—Pontiac, MI, Pontiac Silverdome
February 18—Houston, TX, Rodeo Houston
March 12—Austin, TX, Travis Country Expo Center
March 18—Farmington, CT, Civic Center
March 20—La Crosse, WI, Center Arena
March 21—Peoria, IL, Peoria Civic Center
March 22—Columbia, MO, Hearnes Center
March 23—Lincoln, NE, Pershing Auditorium
March 24—Waterloo, IA, McElroy Auditorium
March 25—Champaign, IL, Assembly Hall
March 27—Moline, IL, Mark of the Quad Cities
March 28—Mankato, MN, Mankato Civic Center
March 29–30—Sioux City, IA, Sioux City Auditorium
March 31—New York, NY, Bramlage Coliseum
April 1—Orlando, FL, Street Party
June 16—Dublin, Ireland, Point Theater

June 17—London, England, Finsbury Park
June 25—Tokyo, Japan, Shibuya, AX
June 28—Sault Ste Marie, MI, Kewadin Casinos
June 29—Uniondale, NY, Nassau Coliseum
July 1—Sault Ste. Marie, MI, Kewadin Casinos
July 2—Milwaukee, WI, Summerfest
July 5—New Orleans, LA, Louisiana Superdome
July 14—Eureka, MO, Six Flags St. Louis
July 18—Albany, NY, Pepsi Arena
July 19—Hartford, CT, Meadows Music Center
July 20—Virginia Beach, VA, Verizon Wireless Amphitheater
July 21—Raleigh, NC, ALLTEL Pavilion at Walnut Creek
July 22—Bristow, VA, Nissan Pavilion at Stone Ridge
July 24—Hershey, PA, Hershey Park Pavilion
July 25—Buffalo, NY, HSBC Arena
July 27—Paso Robles, CA, California Mid-State Fair
July 28—Atlanta, GA, Philips Arena
July 29—St. Louis, MO, Riverport Amphitheater
July 30—Minneapolis, MN, Target Center
August 1—Bonner Springs, KS, Sandstone Amphitheater
August 2—Oklahoma City, OK, Myriad Convention Center
August 3—Selma, TX, Verizon Wireless Amphitheater
August 4—Houston, TX, Compaq Center
August 5—Dallas, TX, Smirnoff Music Center
August 8—Holmdel, NJ, PNC Bank Arts Center
August 9—Camden, NJ, Tweeter Center at the Waterfront
August 10—Mansfield, MA, Tweeter Center for the Performing
   Arts
August 11—Wantagh, NY, Jones Beach Amphitheater
August 13—Toronto, Canada, Air Canada Center
August 14—Columbus, OH, Polaris Amphitheater
August 16—Cincinnati, OH, Riverbend Music Center
August 17—Charlotte, NC, Verizon Wireless Amphitheater
August 18—Tampa, FL, Ice Palace
August 19—Miami, FL, American Airlines Arena
August 21—Antioch, TN, AmSouth Amphitheater
August 22—Cleveland, OH, Gund Arena
August 23—Clarkson, MI, DTE Energy Music Theater
August 24—Burgettstown, PA, Post Gazette Pavilion at Star Lake
August 25—Noblesville, IN, Deer Creek Music Center
August 26—Tinley Park, IL, World Music Theater
August 29—Lancaster, CA, Antelope Valley Fair & Alfalfa Festival
August 30—San Diego, CA, San Diego Sports Arena

August 31—Las Vegas, NV, Mandalay Bay Events Center
September 1—Concord, CA, The Chronicle Pavilion at Concord
September 2—Irvine, CA, Verizon Wireless Amphitheater
September 3—Phoenix, AZ, Desert Sky Pavilion
September 8—Albuquerque, NM, Journal Pavilion
September 9—Denver, CO, Pepsi Center Arena
September 10—Salt Lake City, UT, Utah State Fair
September 21—Honolulu, HI, Blaisdell Arena
September 24—Calgary, Canada, Pengrowth Saddledome
September 25—Bloomsburg, PA, Bloomsburg Fair
September 26—Vancouver, Canada, General Motors Place
October 13–15—Tour of Australia

2002

March 1—Houston, TX, Rodeo Houston
May 7—Okinawa, Japan, Mihama American Village
May 8—Tour of Japan
May 15—Merksem, Belgium, Sportpaleis Antwerpen
May 16—Paris, France, Le Bercy
May 17—Stuttgart, Germany, Hanns Martin Schleyer Halle
May 18—Leipzig, Germany, Messehalle 1
May 20—Koln, Germany, Koln Arena
May 21–23—Rotterdam, Netherlands, Ahoy' Rotterdam
May 25—Copenhagen, Denmark, Forum
May 26—Goteborg, Sweden, Scandinavium
May 28—Stockholm-Globen, Sweden, Stockholm-Globen Arena
May 31—Hamburg, Germany, Sporthalle
June 1—Berlin, Germany, Velodrome
June 3—Frankfurt Am Main, Germany, Festhalle-Ness Frankfurt
June 7–8—London, England, Docklands Arena
June 9—Sheffield, England, Sheffield Arena
June 11—Newcastle, England, Arena
June 13—Manchester, England, Manchester Evening News Arena
June 16–17—Birmingham, England, National Indoor Arena
June 18—London, England, Wembley Arena
June 23—Belfast, Ireland, Odyssey Arena

CAPTIONS AND CREDITS

*All photographs are courtesy of Music World
Entertainment unless otherwise credited.*

CAPTIONS AND CREDITS

ACKNOWLEDGMENTS

Our thanks, our love, and God bless you all

BEYONCÉ

First of all I would like to thank God for His unconditional love and blessings.

Thank you, Momma, for being my best friend and for being such a strong woman, mother, and wife. I hope to be just like you one day.

Daddy, thank you for your courage to fight and your determination to never give up. You are a brilliant businessman, and the best father in the world!

To my sister, Solange, it amazes me how you've grown into a beautiful, talented singer, songwriter, and producer at such an early age. You are truly a SOLO STAR! Words can't express how proud I am of you.

Angela Beyince, you are not only one of my best friends, you are like the big sister I never had! I love you!!!

To Kelly, my sister and my friend, we've spent so many years of our lives together. We've experienced some of life's lowest points and it's highest. And through it all you've always been there for me. I know that God has a great plan for your life. I love you with all of my heart.

Michelle . . . what can I say about the last two years? We've laughed, cried, and accomplished so many things together. I am thankful that God brought you into our lives. I pray that you have a successful year and that all of your dreams come true.

To all of our fans, remember YOU ARE SURVIVORS!

DC3 forever!

KELLY

Thank you, God, for the many blessings and for having Your hands on my life and career. You do it all!

To my mommy, I love you. I'm happy you found your true love. Tina and Mathew Knowles, none of this would be possible without you.

Beyoncé, there is not a day that passes that I don't thank God for you being in my life. You are my sister, my friend, my confidante, but most of all, my blessing. Michelle, these past two years have felt like forever with you. Thank you for all of your hard work, your support, but most of all your love. Beyoncé and Michelle, words cannot express how much I love you. I thank God for making our lives cross and for the sister bond we have. Let's continue to make beautiful music together.

To my truly talented sister Solange, I won't ever take advantage of how important you are in my life. Show the world what you are really about, Solo Star. Angela "My Angel" Beyince, thank you for being the beautiful woman/sister you are; your hard work is truly appreciated.

To all my family, thanks for the continuous support. To my best friend, Barbara, you made the road to life easier to travel. I love you. Angie Phea and Sonja, thank you for being the best sisters. I love you. To the number one Destiny's Child fan, Vernelle Jackson, thanks for believing in us. Ty Hunter and Kim Burse, I love you dearly. And to everyone at Music World Entertainment, your hard work is truly appreciated. Stephanie Gail and Yvette Noel-Schure, I love you so. Wanda Williams, I love you.

Shaya Bryant, we have only just begun. You are doing an incredible job. I love you. You are one of the most beautiful gifts in my life.

MICHELLE

Thank you, God, for this incredible opportunity you have given to me. I never thought in a million years that I would be writing a book!

To my parents: I love you with all of my heart! Thank you for everything!

To all of my family, friends, and teachers: Thank you for helping me become the person I am today.

Beyoncé and Kelly: You both are responsible for helping my dreams come true. I love you both!

Mathew and Tina: I appreciate all of the love and support.

Junella Segura: Without you . . . none of this would have been possible! I love you!

The entire Music World staff: You all do a great job! Thanks!

And anyone I missed . . . THANK YOU!!!